The FOOD Book

Jenny Ridgwell

www.heinemann.co.uk

✓ Free online support
✓ Useful weblinks
✓ 24 hour online ordering

01865 888118

Heinemann

Heinemann is an imprint of Pearson Education Limited, a company incorporated in England and Wales, having its registered office at Edinburgh Gate, Harlow, Essex, CM20 2JE. Registered company number: 872828

www.heinemann.co.uk

Heinemann is a registered trademark of Pearson Education Limited

Text © Pearson Education Limited 2008

First published 2008

ARP impression 98

British Library Cataloguing in Publication Data
A catalogue record for this book is available from the British Library.

ISBN 978 0 435467 95 1

Typeset by Tek-Art
Original illustrations © Pearson Education, 2008
Illustrated by Tek-Art
Cover illustration by Jon Burgerman
Picture research by Helen Reilly and Susi Paz
Printed in Great Britain by Ashford Colour Press Ltd

Acknowledgements
The authors and publisher would like to thank the following organisations for their kind permission to reproduce material:
The Food Standards Agency (p4, p17); The Vegetarian Society (p20); The Fairtrade Foundation (p24); The Soil Association (p26); Organic Farmers & Growers (p26); Duchy Originals (p27); *The Battery Hen* from *The Works* by Pam Ayres, published by BBC Books, Copyright ©Pam Ayres 1992, is reproduced by permission of Sheil Land Associates Ltd (p29); Dove's Farm (p37); Rachel's Organic (p52).

The author and publisher would like to thank the following individuals and organisations for permission to reproduce photographs:
©Magus/Alamy, p8; ©Premier Foods, p11; ©Cut2White, p11; ©LoSalt, p11; ©Alpro UK, p13; ©mediablitzimages (uk) Limited/Alamy, p13; ©iStockphoto/Bobbi Gathings (p16); ©Linda McCartney Foods (p20); ©Gary Roebuck/Alamy, p21; ©Just Kosher (p21); ©Ashley Cooper/Alamy, p22; ©Tim Hill/Alamy, p23; ©Foodfolio/Alamy, p23; ©Mark Boulton/Alamy, p24; ©Peter Titmuss/Alamy, p24; ©iStockphoto/James Goldsworthy, p26; ©iStockphoto/Martin Firus, p32; ©Laurie Strachan/Alamy, p33; ©iStockphoto/LyaC, P34; ©PhotoDisc, p34; ©iStockphoto/Thammarat Kaosombat, p34; ©iStockphoto/MariaBrzostowska, p34; ©Natelle Buklanov/Fotolia.com, p34; ©mediablitzimages (uk) Limited/Alamy, p35; ©Kellogg's, p35; ©Jordans, p35; ©Kellogg's; ©iStockphoto/Gabor Izso, p36; ©mark huls/Fotolia.com, p40; ©Elena Schweitzer/Dreamstime.com, p42; ©iStockphoto/claudia castaldi, p42; ©iStockphoto/Kris Hanke, p42; ©iStockphoto/Ivan Mateev, p42; ©iStockphoto/Mark Strozier, p42; ©Jeff Morgan food and drink/Alamy, p43; ©iStockphoto/Suzannah Skelton, p43; ©Birgit Reitz-Hofmann/Fotolia.com, p44; ©iStockphoto/YinYang, p46; ©iStockphoto/Suzannah Skelton, p46; ©iStockphoto/Steve McCallum, p46; ©iStockphoto/Feng Yu, p46; ©Andy Porter/Dreamstime.com, p46; ©iStockphoto/Suzannah Skelton, p46; ©Nigel Cattlin/Alamy, p46; ©iStockphoto/Ivan Mateev, p46; ©Victor Paul Borg/Alamy, p49; ©iStockphoto/Cynthia Baldauf, p51; ©iStockphoto/Linda & Colin McKie, p55; ©iStockphoto/Juan Monino, p55; ©Corbis, p56; ©Pearson Education Ltd/Tudor Photography, p56; ©jeremybaile/Fotolia.com, p56; ©Helene Sandberg, p58; ©BirdsEye, p60; ©Michaeljung/Dreamstime.com, p61; ©iStockphoto/Konstantin Karchevskiy, p61; ©Superjam (p63); ©Dutto Davide/Dreamstime.com, p66; ©Heinz, p67; ©Barry Bland/Alamy, p67; ©William Nicklin/Alamy, p71, p81; ©Sherman Hines/Alamy, p71; ©iStockphoto/Marcelo Wain, p72; ©Geoffrey Kidd/Alamy, p72; ©Lister, Louise/StockFood UK, p73; ©Pearson Education Ltd/Peter Morris, p75; ©iStockphoto/Felipe Bello, p76; ©Rebel/Fotolia.com, p76; ©Tate & Lyle, p76; © sciencephotos/Alamy, p76; ©mediablitzimages (uk) Limited/Alamy, p76; ©Silverspoon, p76; ©Bon Appetit/Alamy, p77; ©Cut2White, p78; ©Modbury Website, p78; ©Cut2White, p80; ©Helene Rogers/Alamy, p80; ©BirdsEye, p81; ©iStockphoto/Douglas Freer, p81; ©Elena Schweitzer/Dreamstime.com, p81; ©iStockphoto/Cat London, p81; ©vphoto/Fotolia.com, p81; ©Vladimir Popovic/Fotolia.com, p81; ©Pearson Education Ltd/Haddon Davies, p81; ©Cut2White, p81; ©Monika Adamczyk/Dreamstime.com, p81; ©Pearson Education Ltd/Tudor Photography, p82; ©Anthony Mayatt/Dreamstime.com, p82; ©Pearson Education Ltd. Jules Selmes, p82; ©Michael Griffin/Alamy, p84; ©Pearson Education Ltd/MM Studios, p84; ©www.heat2eat.com, p84; ©Steven May/Alamy, p87; ©iStockphoto/Doug Cannell, p91; ©iStockphoto/Remus Eserblom, p91; ©PhotoDisc, p91; ©iStockphoto/Leonid Nyshko, p91; ©iStockphoto/Nell Redmond, p91.

Author acknowledgements

To all the teachers and students who have provided inspiration and help with my work over the years, and to Mark, Annabel and Simon. And thanks to the team of editors who have supported my books.

Every effort has been made to contact copyright holders of material reproduced in this book. Any omissions will be rectified in subsequent printings if notice is given to the publishers.

Websites

There are links to relevant websites in this book. In order to ensure that the links are up to date, that the links work, and that the sites are not inadvertently linked to sites that could be considered offensive, we have made the links available on the Heinemann website at www.heinemann.co.uk/hotlinks. When you access the site, the express code is 7951P.

Contents

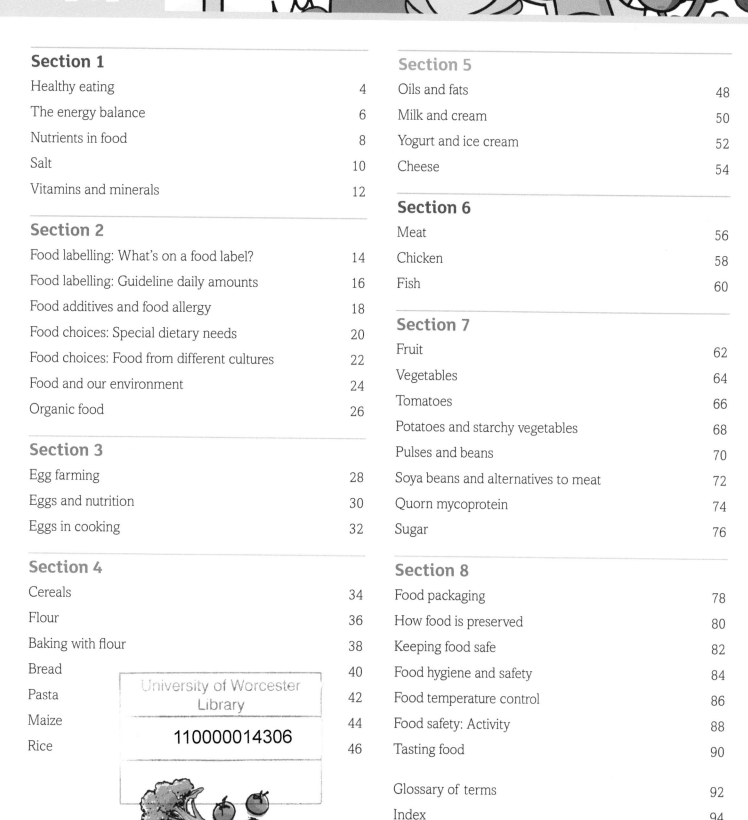

 Hotlinks

Websites included in these sections are available at
www.heinemann.co.uk/hotlinks

Healthy eating

To eat healthily you need to eat a variety of different foods, plenty of fruit and vegetables, and avoid foods which are high in fats and sugars.

These are the UK government's eight guidelines for a healthy diet:

- Enjoy your food.
- Eat a variety of different foods.
- Eat the right amount to be a healthy weight.
- Eat plenty of foods rich in starch and fibre.
- Eat plenty of fruit and vegetables.
- Don't eat too many foods that contain a lot of fat.
- Don't have sugary foods and drinks too often.
- If you drink alcohol, drink sensibly.

Eatwell plate

The Food Standards Agency uses the 'eatwell plate' to show the types and proportions of foods people need for a healthy and well-balanced diet.

This is based on the five food groups:

1 Bread, rice, potatoes, pasta and other starchy foods

2 Fruit and vegetables

3 Milk and dairy foods

4 Meat, fish, eggs, beans and other non-dairy sources of protein

5 Foods and drinks high in fat and/or sugar.

If you choose different foods from the first four groups every day, you eat a wide range of nutrients that your body needs to remain healthy and function properly. Foods in the fifth group – foods and drinks high in fat and/or sugar – are not essential to a healthy diet.

1: Bread, rice, potatoes, pasta and other starchy foods

Other starchy foods include breakfast cereals, oats, noodles, maize, millet and cornmeal, yams and plantain. Beans and pulses can be eaten as part of this group.

2: Fruit and vegetables

This includes fresh, frozen and canned fruit and vegetables, dried fruit and glasses of fruit and vegetable juice.

3: Milk and dairy foods

This includes milk, cheese, yogurt and fromage frais, but does not include butter, eggs and cream.

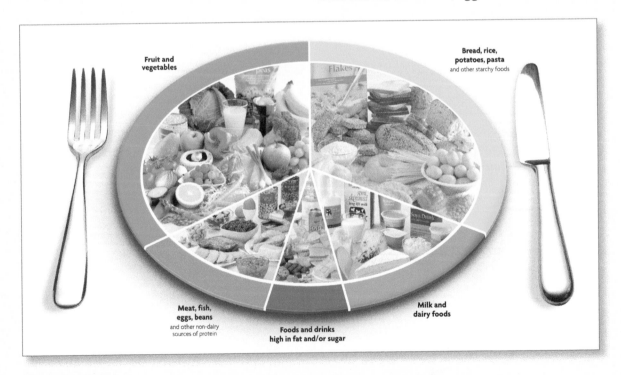

The eatwell plate

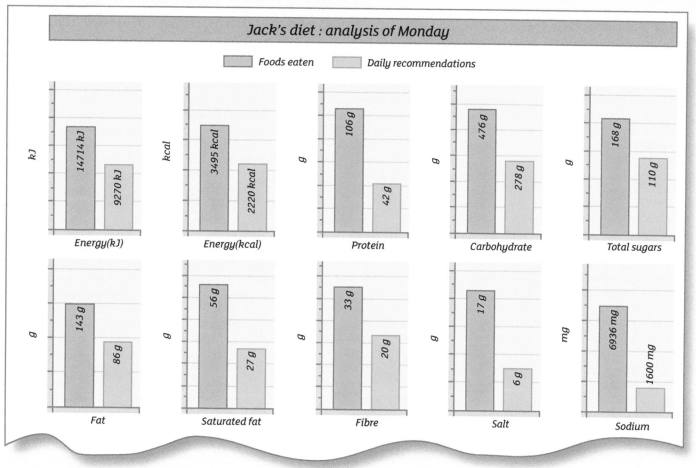

Jack's diet : analysis of Monday

Foods eaten   Daily recommendations

Energy(kJ): 14714 kJ / 9270 kJ
Energy(kcal): 3495 kcal / 2220 kcal
Protein: 106 g / 42 g
Carbohydrate: 476 g / 278 g
Total sugars: 168 g / 110 g
Fat: 143 g / 86 g
Saturated fat: 56 g / 27 g
Fibre: 33 g / 20 g
Salt: 17 g / 6 g
Sodium: 6936 mg / 1600 mg

Daily diet analysis

4: Meat, fish, eggs, beans and other non-dairy sources of protein

Meat includes bacon and salami, and meat products such as sausages, beefburgers and pâté. Fish includes frozen and canned fish such as sardines and tuna, fish fingers and fish cakes. Non-dairy sources of protein include baked beans, pulses and tofu.

5: Foods and drinks high in fat and/or sugar

Foods high in fat include margarine, butter, other spreading fats and 'low-fat' spreads, cooking oils, oil-based salad dressings, mayonnaise, cream, chocolate, crisps, biscuits, pastries, cakes, puddings, ice cream, rich sauces and gravies.

To do

Use a nutritional analysis program such as nutritionprogram.co.uk to find out if your diet is balanced. Enter all the foods you have eaten and check the results. An example analysis is shown above.

Foods and drinks containing sugar include soft drinks, sweets, jam and sugar, as well as foods such as cakes, puddings, biscuits, pastries and ice cream.

@ Hotlinks

Food Standards Agency – information about the eatwell plate

The British Nutrition Foundation

The Nutrition Program – a user-friendly diet analysis tool

? Questions

1 Make a list of all the food and drink you had yesterday. This is a food diary. Draw an empty plate and mark off the different sections. Divide your foods and drink into the sections. Which section has the most foods in it? Is one section empty, or with few foods? If so, write down why you think those foods are missing and discuss them with your group.

2 How do you think your diet could be improved? Give your reasons.

The energy balance

Everything we do needs energy. We need energy not only to move about, but to carry out the body's functions such as heartbeat, breathing and temperature control.

BMR

Our basic metabolic rate (BMR) determines the energy we use when the body is at rest. All of us have different needs. The amount we need depends upon our age, sex, body size and health.

Energy balance

If we eat more food than we need, the excess is changed into fat. If we eat less than we need, and use up energy by taking exercise, the fat stores in the body are burnt as fuel.

- The energy that we get from the food that we eat is called **input**.
- The energy that we use in our daily activities is called **output**.

- Very active people who do physically demanding work or take exercise and run, swim or play sport have a **high energy output**.
- People who sit around all day watching TV or working on the computer have a **low energy output**.
- If the input is more than the output, the body stores the spare energy as fat tissue and you put on weight.

Energy measurement

The energy in our food comes from carbohydrates, fat, protein and alcohol. It is measured in kilojoules (kJ) and kilocalories (kcal) which are shown on food labels.

Food input   Activity output

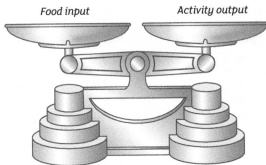

This chart shows the approximate energy use in 20 minutes of activity.

Activity	Time	Kilocalories used
Tennis	20 minutes	150
Dancing	20 minutes	140
Karate	20 minutes	140
Weight training	20 minutes	140
Aerobics	20 minutes	120
Football	20 minutes	160
Sitting	20 minutes	28
Cycling	20 minutes	140
Walking briskly	20 minutes	100
Gardening	20 minutes	66
Jogging	20 minutes	140
Swimming	20 minutes	160
Running	20 minutes	210

This food chart shows the energy (in calories) found in foods,

Food	Kilocalories
Orange juice 200ml	70
Coca cola 330ml	128
Chips, small portion	240
Cream cake	390
Quarter-pounder burger	515
Bag of crisps	166
Spaghetti carbonara	450
Steak pie	690
Lasagne	560
Chocolate cookie	70
Curried beef pattie	460
Jam doughnut	280

Cream cake
390 kcal

Orange juice 200ml
70 kcal

Chips, small portion
240 kcal

Cola 330ml
128 kcal

Steak pie
690 kcal

Quarter-pounder burger
515 kcal

Bag of crisps
166 kcal

Jam doughnut
280 kcal

Energy in foods

Hotlinks

The British Nutrition Foundation

The Nutrition Program – a user-friendly diet analysis tool

To do

You may need a calculator for this activity.

1 Make a list of the exercise you take in one day and the time taken to exercise. Work out how many calories you have used in that time.

2 How would you: a) increase your energy output, b) lower your energy output?

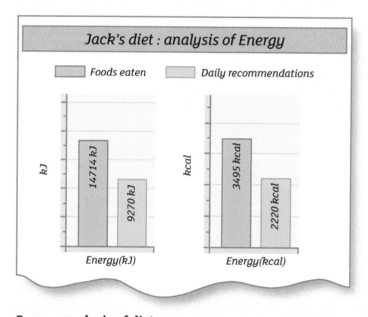

Jack's diet : analysis of Energy

Foods eaten   Daily recommendations

kJ

14714 kJ

9270 kJ

Energy(kJ)

kcal

3495 kcal

2220 kcal

Energy(kcal)

Energy analysis of diet

Further work

Keep a food diary and write down all the food and drink that you consume for a day. Enter this information into a computer program that can analyse your diet, such as nutritionprogram.co.uk. Describe your findings and suggest any changes that you need to make. An example analysis is shown opposite.

Questions

1 Why do we need energy? What happens if our food intake (input) is higher than our daily activities (output)?

2 Describe the activities for a) a day with very low energy output, b) a day with high energy output. Add up the calories used for each day.

3 Choose one of the foods in the food chart above. What activities would you need to do, and for how long, to burn off the calories if you had eaten this food?

The main nutrients in food are carbohydrates, protein and fats. These are called macronutrients.

Carbohydrates

Carbohydrates are a source of energy. Foods rich in carbohydrates include bread, pasta, rice and breakfast cereals, as well as sugar. Simple carbohydrates are known as *sugars* and this energy is released quickly. Complex carbohydrates are starchy foods such as bananas, chickpeas, nuts, potatoes and wholegrain cereals. These foods release energy slowly as they are digested, which makes your energy levels more stable. For a healthy diet, eat more of the complex carbohydrate foods.

Carbohydrate-rich foods

Protein

Protein is needed for growth and repair, and is also a source of energy.

Protein-rich foods include meat, fish, chicken, eggs, beans and nuts. Vegetarians obtain their protein from foods such as pulses – peas, beans, lentils, soya products, grains, pasta, bread, nuts and seeds. A balanced diet should contain all the proteins the body needs.

Protein-rich foods

Fat

Fat is a good source of energy and a source of the essential fatty acids that the body can't make itself, and fat helps the body absorb some vitamins.

All fat is high in calories, so if you are watching your weight, you should limit your fat intake. The total amount of fat you eat should make up no more than 30% of your calories from food.

Foods high in fat include butter, oil, margarine and fried food.

There are two types of fats:

• unsaturated fats

• saturated fats.

Eating too much *saturated* fat can increase blood cholesterol levels and the risk of coronary heart disease. The healthier type of fat is *unsaturated* fat, which can improve cholesterol levels.

Solid fats which contain saturated fat include butter and ghee (clarified butter), lard and coconut cream. Replace saturated fats in cooking with rapeseed or corn oil, which contain unsaturated fat, or just use less of them.

Fats and oils that are liquid at room temperature are more likely to be unsaturated. Food products high in saturated fat include meat, sausages, pies, hard cheese, cakes, pastries, biscuits and food containing coconut or palm oil.

These crisps have less fat

You can buy lower-fat products such as reduced fat spreads and salad dressings, low-fat yogurts, extra-lean minced beef and pork, skimmed and semi-skimmed milks.

Food	% fat
Chocolate	31%
Crisps	33%
Sausage roll	32%
Bombay mix	33%
Salami sausage	44%
Fried bacon	22%
Biscuits	22%

Fibre

Fibre is needed to keep the gut healthy and prevent constipation. Fibre is not digested when we eat it. In the UK most people eat far too little fibre, on average about 12 grams a day or less. Ideally, adults should aim for 18 grams a day, or a little more.

All plant-based foods contain fibre. Good sources of fibre are fruit, vegetables, wholegrain rice and pasta, wholemeal bread, many breakfast cereals, nuts, seeds and bran.

The food label shows the amount of fibre in a food product and you can use a nutritional analysis program to help.

This chart shows foods which are high in fibre. How would you use each one in a recipe? Choose three and describe how you could make them into a recipe or meal.

High fibre foods

To do

Collect some food labels and sort them into groups to show a) foods high and low in sugar, b) foods high and low in fat, c) foods which contain a lot and a little fibre. You can use a nutritional analysis program to find these foods, too.

Food high in Fibre (g)	
Ingredients	g/100g
brussels sprouts, raw	4.1
chapati flour, white	4.1
chestnuts	4.1
chickpeas, canned, drained	4.1
flour, chapati, white	4.1
garlic	4.1
green beans/French beans, boiled in unsalted water	4.1
nut roast	4.1
rissoles, chick pea, fried in sunflower oil	4.1
taro, raw	4.1

Source: The Nutrition Program

Questions

1 Describe a) the functions of carbohydrates, protein and fat; b) three examples of foods which contain each of these nutrients.

2 Why do some people need to reduce the amount of fatty food that they eat? Suggest three ways to cut down on fat.

3 What is the difference between unsaturated and saturated fat? Which foods contain lots of saturated fats?

4 Why is it important to eat foods which contain fibre? Design a meal which contains foods which are good sources of fibre.

Most people eat too much salt, which can raise blood pressure and increase the risk of heart disease and stroke. Salt is sodium chloride and it is the sodium in salt that can raise blood pressure.

Nutrition information				Guideline daily amount		
Typical values (cooked as per instructions)	Per 100g	Per pizza	% based on GDA for women	Women	Men	Children (5-10 years)
Energy	961 kJ	1922 kJ				
	228 kcal	456 kcal	22.8%	2000 kcal	2500 kcal	1800 kcal
			70.2%	45g	55g	24g
Protein	15.8g	31.6g	22.0%	230g	300g	220g
Carbohydrate	25.3g	50.6g	6.0%	90g	120g	85g
of which **sugars**	2.7g	5.4g				
of which starch	22.6g	45.2g	-	70g	95g	70g
Fat	7.1g	14.2g	20.3%	20g	30g	20g
of which **saturates**	1.4g	2.8g	14.0%			
mono-unsaturates	2.2g	4.4g	-	-	-	-
polyunsaturates	3.2g	6.4g	-			
Fibre	5.3g	10.6g	44.2%	24g	24g	15g
Salt	0.8g	1.5g	25.5%	6g	6g	4g
of which sodium	0.3g	0.6g	25.4%	2.4g	2.4g	1.4g

Cutting down on salt

The average salt consumption of adults should be up to 6g a day – a teaspoonful. Most of the salt we eat – 75% – is already in food, rather than added.

The daily recommended maximum for children depends on age:

1 to 3 years: 2g
4 to 6 years: 3g
7 to 10 years: 5g
11 and over: 6g

You need to know how much salt is in the food you eat. Many food labels show the salt or the sodium content in a portion of food, and the percentage of GDA – the guideline daily amount.

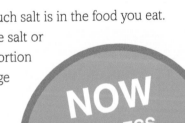

NOW 10% LESS SALT

The label shows that in this pizza, which serves one, there is 1.5g salt, which is over 25% of the GDA.

You can see the amber colour on the chart. Amber is a warning sign, and it means 'Go easy on this food'.

To convert from sodium to salt, multiply the grams of sodium by 2.5.

Levels of salt

The level of salt in food is measured by the amount of salt in 100g of the food.

• High level of salt: more than 1.5g per 100g
• Medium level of salt: 0.3–1.5g per 100g
• Low level of salt: less than 0.3 g per 100g.

Hidden salt

As we have seen, 75% of the salt we eat is already in the foods we buy. Foods high in salt are ready meals, pizzas and sauces such as ketchup. Food companies are trying to cut down on the salt they use.

Reduced salt gravy powder

Reduced salt beans

LoSalt contains 66% less
sodium than ordinary salt

Foods which may be high in salt:

Baked beans, breakfast cereals, bread products, bagels and ciabatta, cooking and pasta sauces, crisps, pizza, ready meals, soup, sandwiches, sausages, tomato ketchup, mayonnaise, bacon, cheese, chips (if salt added), ham, olives, pickles, prawns, salami, salted nuts, soy sauce, stock cubes, yeast extract.

How to reduce salt

• Don't add salt to your foods.

• Try reduced-salt or lower-salt foods.

• Look at food labels and avoid foods which are high in salt.

• If you eat out, watch your choices; for example, try not to add too many salty foods to a pizza.

 Hotlinks

Food Standards Agency – search for information on salt
British Heart Foundation

 To do

Use a nutritional analysis program to find out how much salt is in 100 grams of each of the foods high in salt. When you have the results, list the foods in order, with the highest first. Now discuss which of these foods you would eat a lot, and then think about how you could lower the salt content.

Look at Jack's diet for the day on page 5 – he has eaten over 17 grams of salt!

 Questions

1 What is the most salt that someone of your age should be eating per day?

2 Look at the pizza food label opposite. Is the pizza high, medium or low in salt? Give your reasons.

3 Keep a food diary for a day. Tick the foods you think contain salt. Use a computer program to analyse the amount of salt you have eaten – is it too much? If so, how would you cut down on your salt?

Vitamins and minerals

You have seen the claims on drinks and breakfast cereals: 'Rich in vitamin C', 'Good source of calcium'. Vitamins and minerals are essential for our health.

Vitamins and minerals are called **micronutrients**, which means they are needed in smaller quantities than the macronutrients – protein, carbohydrate and fat. If you eat a variety of foods and a balanced diet you will get most of the nutrients you need.

Foods rich in Vitamin A

Vitamins

There are two groups of vitamins: fat-soluble and water-soluble.

The fat-soluble vitamins – A, D, E, and K – dissolve in fat and are stored in your liver.

- Vitamin A maintains healthy eyes, skin and hair.
- Vitamin D helps form strong bones and teeth.
- Fat-soluble vitamins are found in animal fats such as butter and lard, vegetable oils, dairy foods and oily fish. Margarines can have added vitamin A and D.

The water-soluble vitamins – C and the B-complex vitamins – dissolve in water so that your body can absorb them. Your body can't store these vitamins and any vitamin C or B that your body doesn't use is passed out in your urine. You need a supply of these vitamins every day.

- Vitamin C is required for the structure and maintenance of blood vessels, cartilage, muscle and bone.

- The B group of vitamins help convert food to energy and also help to build healthy nerve tissue.
- These vitamins are found in fruit, vegetables and grain.

Minerals

Minerals are found in the soil and water, and pass into plants and animals that we eat for food. Your body needs small amounts of minerals to grow and stay healthy.

Minerals are necessary for three main reasons:

- building strong bones and teeth
- controlling body fluids
- turning food into energy.

Important minerals include:

calcium   iron   magnesium

phosphorus   potassium   sodium

Foods rich in Vitamin C

Calcium

Calcium is essential for the healthy growth and maintenance of teeth and bones and helps blood clotting and muscle contraction. Good sources of calcium include milk, cheese and other dairy foods, green leafy vegetables, soya beans, tofu, and soya drinks with added calcium.

Foods rich in calcium

Alpro drink is fortified with calcium

Phosphorus

Phosphorus is also essential for healthy bones and teeth and is found in red meat, dairy foods, fish and bread.

Iron

Iron helps to make red blood cells, which carry oxygen around the body. Eat food rich in vitamin C at the same time as you eat food containing non-meat sources of iron to help the body absorb the iron. For example, drink orange juice with a fortified breakfast cereal.

Good sources of iron include liver, meat, beans, nuts, dried fruit, whole grains, fortified breakfast cereals, soybean flour and most dark green, leafy vegetables.

Breakfast cereal fortified with vitamins and minerals

To do

Choose a vitamin or mineral. Your job is to present information on this nutrient to the rest of the group, to show its importance. Each person in the group should present a different nutrient, and at the end the group will vote on which one they think is the best, based on the presentation.

Questions

1 Why are vitamins and minerals important in our diet, and how can you try to make sure you get the nutrients you need?

2 Which are a) the fat-soluble vitamins, b) the water-soluble vitamins? Which foods are good sources of each type of vitamin?

3 Why do we need a) calcium, b) iron in our diet? Which foods are good sources of each mineral?

4 Which foods can have added minerals and vitamins?

Today's food labels contain a lot of vital information. All of the following should be on the label of any packaged food you buy.

❶ List of ingredients

This is the list of ingredients in the food. The largest amount of ingredient by weight is listed first, so in the pizza, the base is the heaviest part (54%). Manufacturers must state what type of additives are used – for example in pizza, an antioxidant: sodium ascorbate. Flavourings must be listed but don't need to be individually named.

❷ Safe storage instructions

This tells you how to store the food and whether it should be kept in the fridge and/or the freezer.

❸ Best-before and use-by dates

'Best-before' dates are used on products that keep for a while. These foods won't go bad after that date, but quality may have deteriorated. 'Use-by' dates are important, because they mean that the food will go off, so you must use it before the date given. You must also make sure you always follow storage instructions.

❹ Nutritional information

This is optional unless a nutrition claim, such as 'low fat' or 'reduced salt', is made. The values must be given per 100g and many products now provide information per portion too.

As well as calories, nutritional information will tell you how much protein, fat and carbohydrate there is in the product. Some products also say how much saturated fat, sugar, fibre and sodium (or salt) is present.

❺ Name and address of the maker, packer or retailer

This information means that you can be sure who is responsible for preparing or selling the food.

A pizza label might include the following information:

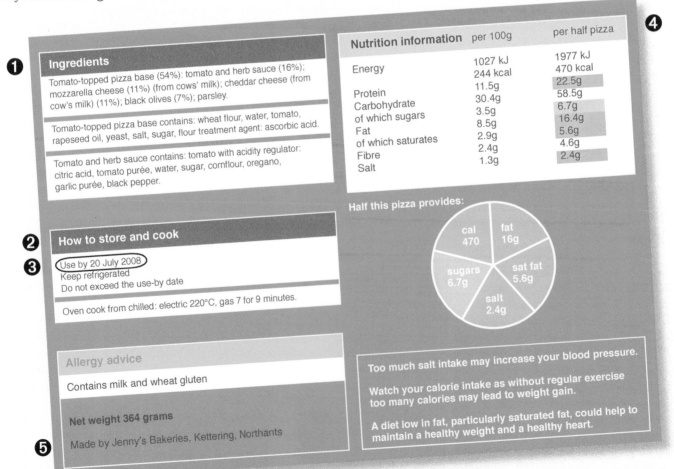

Ingredients

Tomato-topped pizza base (54%): tomato and herb sauce (16%); mozzarella cheese (11%) (from cows' milk); cheddar cheese (from cow's milk) (11%); black olives (7%); parsley.

Tomato-topped pizza base contains: wheat flour, water, tomato, rapeseed oil, yeast, salt, sugar, flour treatment agent: ascorbic acid.

Tomato and herb sauce contains: tomato with acidity regulator: citric acid, tomato purée, water, sugar, cornflour, oregano, garlic purée, black pepper.

How to store and cook

Use by 20 July 2008
Keep refrigerated
Do not exceed the use-by date

Oven cook from chilled: electric 220°C, gas 7 for 9 minutes.

Allergy advice

Contains milk and wheat gluten

Net weight 364 grams

Made by Jenny's Bakeries, Kettering, Northants

Nutrition information	per 100g	per half pizza
Energy	1027 kJ 244 kcal	1977 kJ 470 kcal
Protein	11.5g	22.5g
Carbohydrate	30.4g	58.5g
of which sugars	3.5g	6.7g
Fat	8.5g	16.4g
of which saturates	2.9g	5.6g
Fibre	2.4g	4.6g
Salt	1.3g	2.4g

Half this pizza provides:

cal 470 · fat 16g · sat fat 5.6g · salt 2.4g · sugars 6.7g

Too much salt intake may increase your blood pressure.

Watch your calorie intake as without regular exercise too many calories may lead to weight gain.

A diet low in fat, particularly saturated fat, could help to maintain a healthy weight and a healthy heart.

Case study

Use the pizza label to answer these questions.

1 Make a list of the six most important ingredients in this pizza.

2 Which ingredients do people with food allergies have to watch out for in this pizza?

3 Which ingredients in this pizza contain salt? How would you lower the salt content?

4 What would you eat with this pizza to make it a healthy meal? Give reasons for your answer.

5 How should the pizza be stored and cooked?

6 Draw and label the pizza to show the main ingredients in each part.

7 What ingredients are used to provide a) protein; b) carbohydrate; c) fibre?

8 What additives are used in the pizza?

Hotlinks

Food Standards Agency

BBC Food – search for 'labelling'

To do

Design your own food label for your favourite recipe. You can do this by hand or use a computer program to help.

Remember:

- include all the information categories shown opposite
- make it attractive so customers are encouraged to read it
- make it clear so it is easy to understand.

Guideline daily amounts (GDAs) are a guide to show the recommended daily levels of certain nutrients needed to maintain good health.

Guideline daily amounts

GDA for each day	women	men	children 5–10 years
Kilocalories	2000	2500	1800
Sugars	90g	120g	85g
Fat	70g	95g	70g
of which saturates	20g	30g	20g
Fibre AOAC	24g	24g	15g
Fibre NSP	18g	18g	11g
Salt	6g	6g	4g

	trace	trace
of which saturates	0.4g	2.5g
Fibre	trace	0.1g
Sodium		

Each tablespoon contains the equivalent of **trace salt**.

Guideline daily amounts for a typical adult

	Guideline daily amount	Each tablespoon	% guideline daily amount
Calories	2000kcal	14kcal	1%
Sugar	90g	2.0g	2%
Fat	70g	trace	<1%
Saturated fat	20g	trace	<1%
Salt	6g	trace	<1%

For further information, please visit: www.tesco.com/health

Guideline daily amounts on a food label

Many food labels show the guideline daily amounts

Traffic light system

The traffic light system on food labels shows you whether food is high, medium or low in fat, saturated fat, sugars and salt. This helps you make healthy choices when shopping.

Red = high: eat small amounts, or just occasionally

Amber = medium: OK most of the time

Green = low: a healthier choice

	Green (low)	Amber (medium)	Red (high)	By portion
Fat	less than 3g in 100g	more than 3g but less than 20g in 100g	more than 20g in 100g	more than 21g in portion
Saturates	less than 1.5g in 100g	more than 1.5g but less than 5g in 100g	more than 5g in 100g	more than 6g in portion
Total sugars	less than 5g in 100g	more than 5g but less than 15g in 100g	more than 15g in 100g	more than 18g in portion
Salt	less than 0.3g in 100g	more than 0.3g but less than 1.5g in 100g	more than 1.5g in 100g	more than 2.4g in portion

The traffic light system is really useful for ready meals, sausages, pies and pizzas to show if they are high in fat, sugar and salt. But these foods could be eaten with salad, and are part of a whole day's diet, which includes other foods such as fruits and vegetables. If you worked out the traffic lights for the whole meal, then each portion would not be in the red.

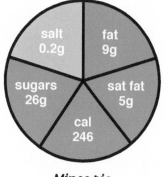

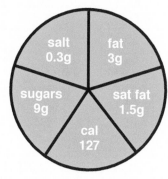

Mince pie   *Iced bun*

Examples of traffic light labelling for a mince pie and an iced bun

- Each mince pie provides:

  246 kcal, fat 8.8g, sat fat 5.1g, salt 0.2g, total sugars 26.3g

- One iced bun provides:

  127 kcal, fat 3.1g, sat fat 1.5g, salt 0.3g, total sugars 8.9g

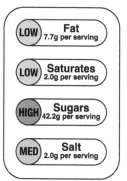

Label A   **Label B**

Questions

1 Suggest three food products which might have the traffic light labels A and B. Give reasons for your choice.

2 Draw your own traffic lights for the foods in the table below which gives the nutrition for 100g of each food.

	Apple sauce	Bacon	Fromage frais	Vegetable crisps
Fat	0.1 g	19 g	2.9 g	36 g
Saturated fat	0 g	9 g	1.9 g	4 g
Sugar	27 g	0.1 g	12.5 g	30 g
Salt	0.1 g	4.8 g	0.04 g	1.2 g

To do

Use a nutritional analysis program to find the nutritional value of a recipe of your choice. Work out the GDA and traffic light ratings (see above) for the product.

Food additives and food allergy

There are many different kinds of food additives, serving different purposes. Additives can only be used in foods if they are fully tested to make sure they are safe to eat.

Contain preservatives

May contain flavours, colours, sweeteners

May contain emulsifiers and flavours

May contain preservatives

Sausages *Fizzy pop* *Low-fat spread* *Ice-cream* *Bread*

Types of additives

Preservatives help stop food from spoiling and 'going off'. Micro-organisms such as bacteria, yeast and mould make changes in food which can lead to food poisoning.

Antioxidants stop oils and fats becoming sour and tasting stale. They are added to meat pies and salad dressings.

Gelling agents give food the correct texture and consistency.

Emulsifiers help to mix foods which contain fats, oils and water which would normally separate. They are used in low-fat spreads, ice cream and salad dressings to give a smooth texture.

Flavours give extra colour to food. They are added to soft drinks, margarine, ice cream and sauces.

Flavour enhancers such as monosodium glutamate bring out the flavour of savoury and sweet food without adding flavour of their own.

Colours make the food look more attractive to eat. Colours are often added to soft drinks, sweets and ice cream.

Sweeteners replace sugar in low-calorie foods and provide sweetness without calories. Aspartame and saccharin are sweeteners added to drinks, yogurts and chewing gum.

Acids give a sharpness to foods. Citric acid is used to flavour fizzy drinks.

Additives are not used in all processed foods. Canned foods don't need preservatives because the canning process uses high temperatures to preserve the food.

Is hyperactivity linked to food colours?
Government advice:

'Parents of children showing signs of hyperactivity are advised that eliminating certain artificial food colours from their diets might have some beneficial effects on their behaviour. If parents are concerned about any additives they should remember that, by law, food additives must be listed on the label so they can make the choice to avoid the product if they want to.'

Food allergy

Allergic reactions are caused by substances in the environment known as **allergens**. Peanuts, milk and eggs are common food allergens.

Anyone who suspects he or she has a food allergy should see a doctor and take an allergy test.

Food labelling

All pre-packed food has a list of ingredients. Food labels show allergens, so people with food allergies can make safe choices. Common food allergies are caused by peanuts, tree nuts such as almonds and hazelnuts, crustaceans such as prawns, milk, eggs, sesame seeds, soya, celery, fish, and cereals with gluten, such as wheat.

Nut alert for a breakfast cereal recall

A batch of Bloggos Cereals has been taken off the shop shelves due to cross-contamination with peanuts. The company advises peanut allergy sufferers not to eat any of this product and to return the pack top with date code to get a full refund.

Not suitable for Nut allergy sufferers

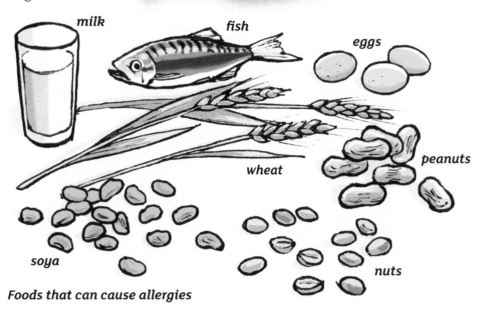

milk fish eggs wheat peanuts soya nuts

Foods that can cause allergies

 Allergy advice   Contains: milk, wheat gluten & soya.

Allergy advice label

 To do

Use the Internet to find out more about food additives and food allergies. Try to find up-to-date news articles. Prepare a short presentation.

 Hotlinks

The Food and Drink Federation

Food Additives and Ingredients Association

Allergy UK – a medical charity dealing with allergies

The Anaphylaxis Campaign – a charity set up to help people with life-threatening allergies

 Questions

1 Why are food additives used in food products? How can you find out if food additives are used in a food product?

2 What type of additive is added to food to a) help it keep longer, b) stop the fats and oils going sour, c) mix oils and water, d) add sweetness, e) make food thicker?

3 What is a flavour enhancer?

4 What advice would you give to someone who thinks he or she has a food allergy?

5 What are the main foods which cause food allergies? How do you know if they are in a food product?

Food labels can show if a food meets special dietary needs, such as vegetarian, Kosher or Halal.

The Vegetarian Society Symbol shows that the food product has been accredited by the society

Prepared dishes suitable for vegetarians are popular

Vegetarian

A vegetarian does not eat any meat, poultry, game, fish, shellfish or crustacea, or any products made from these foods, so vegetarians need to read food labels carefully and check whether vegetarian symbols are on the packs.

A vegetarian eats a diet of grains, pulses, nuts, seeds, vegetables and fruits and may eat dairy products and eggs.

Types of vegetarian

Lacto-ovo-vegetarians eat dairy products and eggs. This is the most common type of vegetarian diet.

Lacto-vegetarians eat dairy products but not eggs.

Vegans do not eat dairy products, eggs, or any other animal product.

Food ingredients that vegetarians must avoid

- Gelatine is made from boiling animal bones and products. It is used in low-fat spreads, desserts, and sweets.
- Suet and lard are animal fats, and some margarines are made with animal fat.
- E120 cochineal is a red colouring made from crushed beetles – therefore an animal product.
- Some cheeses are made using animal rennet; most cheese uses vegetarian rennet.

A varied diet

It is possible to obtain all the nutrients you need by eating a varied vegetarian diet. Instead of eating meat, poultry and fish, vegetarians obtain protein from the following foods.

- Nuts: brazils, almonds, cashews, walnuts, pinenuts.
- Seeds: sesame, pumpkin, sunflower.
- Pulses: peas, beans, lentils, peanuts.
- Grains/cereals: wheat, barley, rye, oats, millet, maize, rice.
- Soya products: tofu, textured vegetable protein, veggie burgers, soya milk.
- Dairy products: milk, cheese, yogurt (for lacto-vegetarians).
- Eggs (for lacto-ovo-vegetarians).

Kosher

Kosher food is food that meets Jewish dietary laws, or *kashrut*, which comes from the Hebrew word for 'fit' or 'proper'. Kosher food must follow special rules. For example:

- pork, shellfish and some other animal foods are non-kosher
- meat and fowl must be slaughtered in a special way to be kosher
- meat and dairy products may not be made or eaten together.

Halal

Halal food is prepared according to Islamic principles. This means that there is no alcohol or pork in the product, and if meat is used, the animal was slaughtered according to an Islamic method.

Case study: Haribo

Sweets maker Haribo has launched a Halal variety of its sweets, aimed specifically at Muslim children. The fruit-flavoured jellies do not contain gelatine, which is unacceptable to Muslims because it is made from animal products forbidden under Islamic law. Alcohol-based colourings and flavourings have also been taken out. An Imam from the Muslim Association visited the factory to check on the manufacturing process and that every ingredient had been given a Halal food certificate. The packaging has a green sticker with the word *Halal* written in English and Arabic.

A Halal meat shop

To do

1 Plan a day's meals which are suitable for a) a vegetarian who eats eggs and milk, b) a vegan.

2 Explain how you have provided protein in the day's meals.

3 Test out your plans using a nutritional analysis program to see whether they meet nutritional needs. If not, make some changes and test again.

Kosher delivery van

Further work

Work in small groups and use the Internet to find out more about one of the following, then create a presentation of your work: a) Kosher food; b) Halal food.

Hotlinks

The Vegetarian Society

Just Kosher – the UK's largest online Kosher superstore

Questions

1 What are the names of the different types of vegetarian, and what foods does each type of vegetarian avoid eating?

2 Explain what is meant by Kosher and Halal food.

Many people from different cultures live in Britain today and supermarkets are keen to supply their favourite foods.

Foods of the world

The large supermarket chain Asda has a special team of food buyers who run the World Food Hub and are responsible for finding foods to meet local demand.

New companies are producing food for customers from different cultures, and growers experiment with exotic vegetables. Here are some examples of new foods from around the world.

Poland

Polish food has been the fastest-growing ethnic food range ever launched in Britain. Many supermarkets stock Polish items in stores where there is a large demand for specialist food from the biggest community of people from Eastern Europe.

Popular foods include borsch, meatballs, pickled vegetables, sauerkraut, stuffed cabbage, zurek soup, bigos and golabki. Most of the foods are made in Poland and imported for sale.

India

Patak's is a company famous for making award-winning curry sauces, curry pastes and chutneys, naan bread and pappadums. Patak's ingredients make it easy to prepare authentic Indian dishes at home. The company supplies most of Britain's 8,000 Indian restaurants with ingredients, and has large food factories in the UK.

Patak's makes a range of chutneys, sauces and pastes

The Caribbean

The range of Afro-Caribbean foods you can find in shops is also expanding. Ready meals include salt fish and calaloo, ackee and cassava chips. Sweet potatoes, plantains, yams and fruits from around the world are easy to buy.

Jamaican patties

Delicious Jamaican patties are sold in supermarkets and West Indian stores. There are different varieties including beef, lamb, chicken, vegetable and salt fish, and you can get patties made with Halal meat.

New vegetables

Chinese stir fries use a range of exotic vegetables, but now pak choi and beansprouts are grown in the UK and have become common vegetables for all sorts of cooking.

Look at the following supermarket websites to see the range of foods they offer from around the world:

 Hotlinks

Sainsbury's

Asda

Tesco

Popular Polish dishes include Golabki

Ackee and saltfish is a traditional Jamaican dish

 To do

Use the Internet to find out about food from another culture. You could search the supermarket sites and discover their ready meals, new breads, vegetables and fruits.

 Questions

1 Think about the foods you use at home. Make a list of those that come from other countries.

2 Describe how these foods are used.

Food and our environment

People are getting more concerned about the effect of global food production on our environment, and on the people who grow and harvest our food. Some organisations give information on food labels to show us the challenges ahead.

Carbon footprints for food

A carbon footprint is the total amount of carbon dioxide (CO_2) and other greenhouse gases emitted over the life cycle of a product. The Carbon Trust has a carbon label which shows the carbon footprint of a product.

For example, Innocent Drinks, which makes smoothies, and Walkers Crisps both have carbon labels. The label for mango and passion fruit smoothie was developed by the Carbon Trust to show the carbon footprint for a 250ml bottle. To use the label, the company must

Carbon footprint label

reduce its carbon footprint in the next two years and look at all production processes to reduce the emission of greenhouse gases.

Fairtrade

Fair trade is about giving a fair deal to people who work in some of the poorest countries of the world. Businesses work with suppliers to make sure that the workers are treated well and are given a fair wage. The Fairtrade mark is found on products which meet internationally recognised standards. You will find the Fairtrade logo on packets of coffee, tea and sugar and lots of fruits such as avocados, bananas and pineapples.

The Fairtrade mark

Case study: The banana story

Workers on banana plantations are often paid low wages, with poor working conditions, but things are changing. One in five bananas from the Windward Islands in the Caribbean now carry the Fairtrade mark, and increasing sales are helping Windward Islands banana farmers to survive.

The farmers work together, holding weekly meetings to make business decisions such as reducing the use of chemicals in their farming, and to help each other. Thanks to the premium which comes with Fairtrade sales, school furniture has been purchased, which means that local children can attend class all day rather than for just part of the day; street lights have been installed; farm access roads have been renovated; and a pre-school building has been built so small children no longer have to walk four miles a day to school.

Bananas from the Windward Islands

Where do they come from?

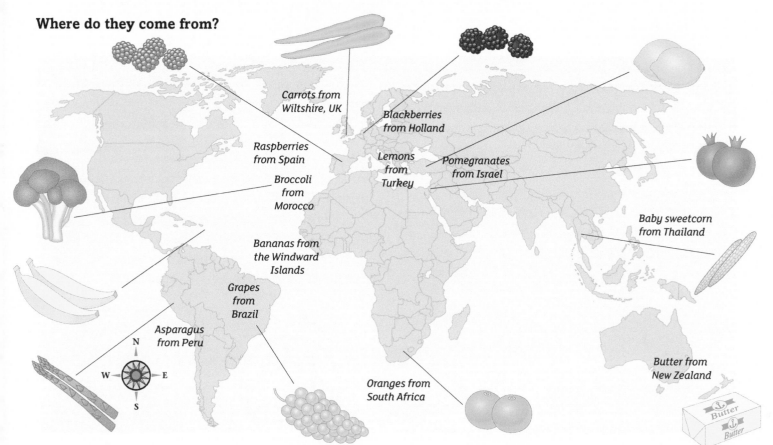

Carrots from Wiltshire, UK

Blackberries from Holland

Raspberries from Spain

Lemons from Turkey

Pomegranates from Israel

Broccoli from Morocco

Baby sweetcorn from Thailand

Bananas from the Windward Islands

Grapes from Brazil

Asparagus from Peru

Butter from New Zealand

Oranges from South Africa

N
W   E
S

Food miles

The term 'food miles' makes us think about the distance our food travels from field to plate and the environmental impact of transporting foods around the world.

For example, we like to eat strawberries all year round, so in the winter these fruits are flown in from warmer parts of the world where they are grown. Years ago, we used to eat fruit and vegetables only when they were in season locally, but now 95% of UK fruit is imported from other countries.

Some people question whether food miles matter. Research shows that tomatoes grown in Spain and brought to the UK may have a lower carbon footprint than tomatoes grown in the UK. Spain has a warmer climate, and in the UK greenhouses which grow tomatoes are heated during colder months, which increases the energy used.

To do

Visit your local supermarket or look at its website and make a list of fruits and vegetables available and where they come from.

@ Hotlinks

The Fairtrade Foundation

Innocent Drinks

The Carbon Trust

Questions

1 Explain what is meant by 'carbon footprint', and why it is useful for food companies to show this information on the label.

2 What are your views about fair trade in food products? Make three comments.

3 Using an atlas for reference if necessary, draw a line on the map to show the journey for each of the food products as they travel to the UK. List the journeys in order, starting with the shortest food-mile journey.

4 Explain why you think each product comes from where it does. For example, 'It is too cold to grow oranges in the UK, so they must come from hotter places such as South Africa'.

Sales of organic food in supermarkets and farmers' markets are rapidly increasing.

What is organic food?

Any food labelled organic must meet strict standards for the use of pesticides, additives, animal welfare and sustainability. Organic farms use few chemicals and most pesticides are banned. When they are used, they are carefully controlled.

The organic movement aims for food that is produced as 'naturally' as possible, free from trans fats, GMOs (genetically modified organisms), and most additives. In the UK, the Soil Association is the main organisation which checks on farms and food products to make sure they meet its standards.

How are organic animals treated?

To get an organic certificate, farmers have to keep animals in certain ways – they must have access to the outdoors on organic land, and the numbers in the herd are controlled. Chickens have to be free range and able to scratch about outdoors and get plenty of sunlight.

Organic farmers try to avoid using antibiotics on animals, although these are allowed if the health of the animal is at risk. But while on antibiotics, products from that animal, such as its meat or milk, cannot be sold as organic.

Why do people buy organic foods?

People who eat organic food think that it tastes better and is healthier. They may want to avoid foods which are produced using artificial chemical fertilisers and pesticides. Organic farming is friendly to the environment and encourages biodiversity, as the lack of herbicides and pesticides helps increase the range of birds, insects and plants.

Organic pig farming

Why does organic food cost more?

Organic food production is more labour-intensive than other farming; crops are grown less often in the same piece of ground; and animals are held at lower stocking densities. The controls placed on organic production add to the costs of organic seeds and animal feeds, which cost more than non-organic versions.

Case study: Duchy Originals

The Prince of Wales has an organic farm, called the Duchy Home Farm, which aims to create a sustainable system for farming and food production, and protect the health of the soil, the environment and wildlife for generations to come. In 1986, the Duchy Home Farm gained organic status and research began to create a food and drinks company based on sustainable food production, called Duchy Originals.

After hundreds of trials the perfect recipe for a crisp, thin oat biscuit was developed. The biscuits are baked using natural ingredients, with no artificial colours, flavouring or sweeteners.

DUCHY ORIGINALS
O R G A N I C

OATEN BISCUITS
Baked with organic oats & wheat

PROFITS DONATED TO THE PRINCE OF WALES'S
CHARITABLE FOUNDATION

DUCHY ORIGINALS
O R G A N I C
16 ORGANIC OATEN BISCUITS
INGREDIENTS: ORGANIC OATS (68%), ORGANIC BUTTER (13%), ORGANIC RAW CANE SUGAR, ORGANIC WHEAT FLOUR (8%), SEA SALT*, RAISING AGENT (SODIUM BICARBONATE)*.
*APPROVED NON ORGANIC INGREDIENT. STORE IN A COOL DRY PLACE. BEST BEFORE SEE BASE. NOT SUITABLE FOR NUT ALLERGY SUFFERERS.

Hotlinks

The Soil Association – a leading environmental charity

Organic Farmers & Growers Ltd

Duchy Originals

Questions

1 Explain why you think some people choose to buy and eat organic food. Would you choose it? Give reasons for your answer.

2 What farming methods are used for organic animals?

3 Why is most organic food more expensive than food produced by other farming methods?

4 Use the information on Duchy Organic Oaten Biscuits to answer these questions:

a) Which biscuit ingredients come from outside the UK? Give reasons for your answer.

b) Which ingredients are not organic? What is their purpose in the recipe?

Egg Farming

In the UK we eat nearly 10,500 million eggs a year – that's nearly 173 eggs each. About 83% of our eggs come from the UK and 17% are imported.

Lion Quality mark

The Lion Quality mark shows that eggs have been produced to the highest food safety standards. About 85% of UK eggs are produced to this standard, which states that:

- hens that lay Lion Quality eggs are vaccinated against salmonella enteritidis
- there are increased hygiene controls and salmonella testing throughout the production system
- a best-before date and Lion logo must be printed on the egg shell and the egg box.

Salmonella are a type of food poisoning bacteria which are found in poultry and eggs. These foods must be handled carefully to avoid causing illness. Vaccination and strict hygiene controls reduce the risk of food poisoning from eggs.

How are eggs farmed?

There are about 30 million egg-laying hens in the UK, and they lay 310 eggs a year, on average:

- 66% laying cage
- 27% free range
- 7% barn.

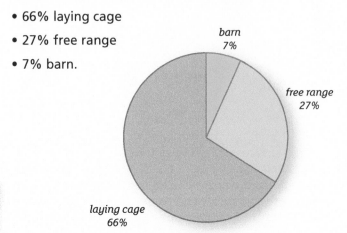

Egg farming in the UK

Laying cages

This is the most common method of egg production, and is also known as battery farming.

The chickens are kept indoors in cages with sloping, wire-mesh floors, and the eggs roll away from the birds. There are troughs with food for the chickens and an automatic water supply. The temperature and light are controlled, so the hens lay throughout the year.

Three ways to farm eggs: laying cages, free range, and barn

Free range

Free-range hens are allowed outside so they can roam about freely during daylight and live in a henhouse at night. The hens have a varied diet, as they peck the plants as well as eating their feed. Free-range hens are at risk from predators such as foxes, and they need to have their beaks clipped to stop them from pecking each other.

Barn

In the barn system, the hen house has lots of perches and feeders at different levels. The hens can move about freely inside, and are protected against predators. Light is controlled to give the best day length throughout the year, and at the end of the egg-laying period the house is completely cleared and disinfected. Birds need their beaks clipped to prevent pecking.

Organic eggs

These hens are always free range, live on organic land and are fed an organic diet.

Imported eggs contain salmonella

A survey has shown that millions of imported eggs are contaminated with salmonella, which causes serious food poisoning and even death. The Food Standards Agency said consumers can protect themselves by making sure that these eggs are cooked thoroughly, with a solid yolk. This is important for vulnerable groups, such as the elderly, babies and toddlers, and pregnant women, and people who are already unwell. The European Commission has set targets to reduce salmonella in laying flocks and introduce compulsory vaccination in countries with a high rate of contaminated flocks.

Organic eggs

Extract from *The Battery Hen* by Pam Ayres

Oh, I am a battery hen,
  On me back there's not a germ,
I never scratched a farmyard,
  And I never pecked a worm,
I never had the sunshine,
  To warm me feathers through.
Eggs I lay. Every day.
  For the likes of you. […]

But it's no life, for a battery hen,
  In me box I'm sat,
A funnel stuck out from the side,
  Me pellets comes down that,
I gets a squirt of water,
  Every half a day,
Watchin' with me beady eye,
  Me eggs, roll away. […]

I lays them in a funnel,
  Strategically placed,
So that I don't kick 'em,
  And let them go to waste,
They rolls off down the tubing,
  And up the gangway quick,
Sometimes I gets to thinkin'
  'That could have been a chick!'

Hotlinks

The British Egg Information Service

To do

1 How do chickens produce eggs? Find out about the egg-laying cycle.

2 What other birds' eggs do we eat? Find some recipes using these eggs.

Eggs and nutrition

Eggs are one of the most nutritious foods we can buy, and good value for money. There is no recommended limit on how many eggs we should eat – an egg a day is healthy.

Eggs contain:

- easily digestible protein needed for growth
- essential vitamins A, D, E and B groups – but no vitamin C
- essential minerals iron, phosphorus and zinc
- low amounts of saturated fat, and only 80–90 kcal each.

Researchers have found that eating eggs for breakfast can help you feel full during the morning. This is useful for people wanting to lose weight as it stops them from snacking on calorie-rich foods.

How do you know when an egg was laid?

Find the best-before date on the egg or the box. Take off 28 days to find the laying day.

Is a brown egg better than a white egg?

No, the taste and nutrition of an egg depend on the diet and health of the hen that laid it, not the colour of the shell.

Parts of an egg

A hen's egg is 10% shell, 60% white, 30% yolk. The egg shell is very strong but also thin and porous. When you crack an egg, you can see the thin membrane that protects the inside of the egg.

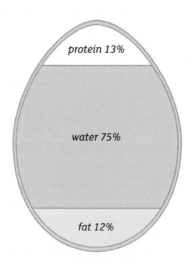

protein 13%

water 75%

fat 12%

Contents of an egg

At the blunt end of the egg is an air pocket and this pocket gets bigger as the egg gets older.

The egg white, called *albumen*, surrounds the yolk, and is a thin solution made up of water, protein, minerals and carbohydrate. The yolk is held in place with two cord-like strands called *chalazae*. The yolk is a rich source of protein and iron. On the yolk the germinal disc contains some of the hen's DNA, and the young bird would develop here if the egg was fertilised. Eggs sold in the shops are not fertilised.

Eggs are sold in four different sizes: small, medium, large and very large. Large eggs are used in recipes.

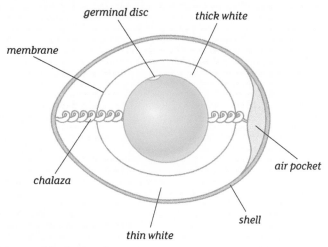

germinal disc *thick white*

membrane

air pocket

chalaza

shell

thin white

Parts of an egg

Food safety

Egg allergy is most common in children under 12 months. Few children are allergic to egg after the age of six, though in some cases this allergy can persist to adult life, especially for people with a family history of allergy.

⊙ **Allergy advice** | May contain egg

Eggs, like any protein-rich food, need to be handled carefully.

- Store eggs at a constant temperature below 20°C.
- Store away from strong-smelling food – eggs are porous and absorb smells.
- Store away from raw meat – cross-contamination from the meat may occur.
- Wash your hands before and after handling eggs.
- Never use dirty, cracked or broken eggs.
- Do not re-use left-over egg dishes.

 To do

Use the Internet to find:

- ten egg dishes that can be served for breakfast or brunch
- ways in which caterers use large quantities of eggs in their cooking.

Eggs for caterers

Chefs can buy eggs ready shelled, in liquid, frozen and dried form. Omelettes can be bought ready-cooked and hard-boiled eggs are cooked and shelled to use in products such as Scotch eggs and sandwiches.

The latest innovation for egg products is the 'extended shelf-life' egg. Liquid egg is pasteurised at a high temperature for a short time and it has a shelf life of approximately one month.

@ **Hotlinks**

Noble Foods – the UK's biggest supplier of eggs and egg products

American Egg Board

 Questions

1 Why do eggs make a good breakfast food? List three breakfast dishes that can be made from eggs. Describe how they are made and how long they take to cook.

2 If an egg box is labelled 'Best before 20 November 2008', when were the eggs laid?

3 Draw and label a cross-section of an egg. What is the value of each part?

4 What size egg is used in recipes?

5 Give three tips on storing and handling eggs safely.

6 Give three reasons why caterers might buy their eggs ready-shelled.

Eggs are a very useful cooking ingredient. Without them we couldn't make omelettes, cakes, noodles, ice creams and sauces.

Main meals

Eggs are used to make main meal dishes such as omelette, frittata, and quiche.

Other uses for eggs

- **Binding:** Eggs are used to bind or stick other ingredients together in dishes such as beefburgers, fishcakes and croquettes.

- **Coating:** A fishcake can be dipped in beaten egg then coated with flour or breadcrumbs. The egg protects the ingredients inside during frying.

- **Glazing:** Eggs are used to glaze savoury pastry such as cheese straws and bread dough to make it golden when baked.

- **Thickening:** Eggs can thicken custards, flan, quiches, soups and sauces. Egg is a liquid food which contains protein and this thickens with gentle heat. Eggs thicken as you make omelette and scrambled egg.

- **Trapping air:** Eggs can trap air when they are whisked or beaten. This is used for soufflés and cakes such as sponges. Eggs whites trap air to make meringues.

Eggs have many uses in cooking

 Experiment

You will need an egg, plate, knife, fork, bowl, butter, and pepper.

- Crack an egg onto a plate – make sure the yolk does not break.

- Look at the different parts: the thick and thin white, egg yolk, chalaza, and germ.

- Compare your egg with others in the group. Is there a difference in the colour of the yolks and whites?

- Look inside the shell and see the air sac and membrane lining of the shell.

- Make the egg into something to eat – put the egg in a bowl and beat with a fork until it is all mixed up. Add a little butter and pepper. Place the bowl in the microwave and cook for a minute. Take out and stir. Cook a little longer until the egg is firm. Serve on hot, buttered toast.

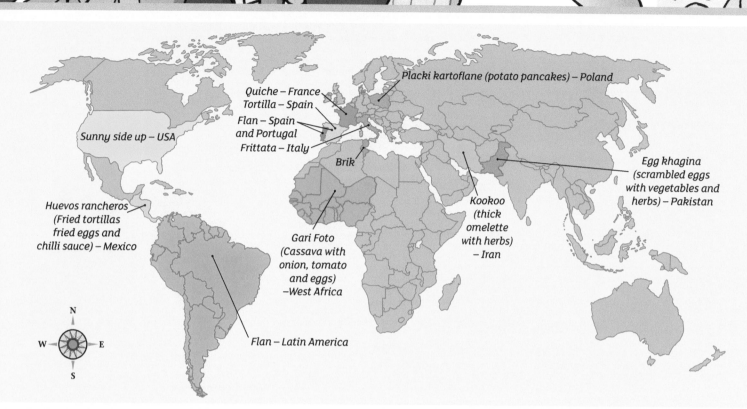

Quiche – France
Tortilla – Spain
Flan – Spain and Portugal
Frittata – Italy

Placki kartoflane (potato pancakes) – Poland

Sunny side up – USA

Brik

Egg khagina (scrambled eggs with vegetables and herbs) – Pakistan

Huevos rancheros (Fried tortillas fried eggs and chilli sauce) – Mexico

Gari Foto (Cassava with onion, tomato and eggs) –West Africa

Kookoo (thick omelette with herbs) – Iran

N
W – E
S

Flan – Latin America

Eggs around the world

Eggs around the world

Eggs are used for many famous dishes around the world.

Chinese thousand-year-old egg

This egg is not really a thousand years old. The egg is packed inside a mixture of straw, lime, salt, clay and ash and left for a month to preserve it. The yolk and white turn dark brown and it is eaten as a delicacy.

To do

Find out how some of the dishes listed above are made. Use the Internet to find ten more popular egg dishes from around the world. Try making one of your favourites.

You could try the Wikipedia website for recipe research.

Questions

1 Explain the function of the egg in each of these dishes:

   a) on top of pastry for sausage rolls

   b) in a quiche – an egg dish in pastry

   c) beaten eggs to make a sponge cake

   d) mixed with chopped vegetables to make a veggie burger

   e) a piece of fish dipped in egg and flour before frying.

2 Add three egg dishes of your own to the map of the world above.

Cereals

Cereals are plant seeds and are a valuable source of starch, which we use for food energy. Cereals provide protein for growth and the whole grain is a good source of fibre, which helps our digestive system.

Staple food

Cereals are called a *staple food* because they form the main part of the diet for many people of the world.

Maize, rice and wheat are the main cereals grown, making up 88% of world grain production.

This chart shows the main cereal crops of the world.

- Maize is a staple food for Africa, South America and Mexico.
- Rice is a staple food for China, Indonesia and Asia.
- Wheat is a staple food for Northern Europe and North America.

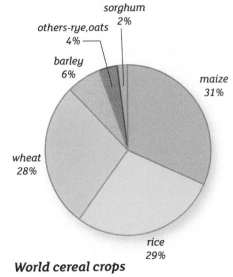

sorghum 2%
others-rye,oats 4%
barley 6%
maize 31%
wheat 28%
rice 29%

World cereal crops

What do we use cereals for?

Wheat – bread, pasta, couscous, pastry, biscuits

Maize – cornflour, breakfast cereal, polenta

Rice – rice, rice flour

Oats – porridge, flapjacks, bread

Rye – bread

Breakfast cereals

Breakfast cereals are the most popular breakfast food in the UK and they are made from different types of cereal.

Breakfast is an important meal because it 'breaks the fast' when we haven't eaten for many hours. Nearly half of the people in the UK don't have breakfast, but breakfast provides us with energy that we need to start the day, and research has shown that eating breakfast can help us concentrate at work.

Breakfast cereals are a good source of carbohydrates for energy and fibre. Many breakfast cereals are fortified with vitamins and minerals, so are important sources of iron, folic acid and vitamins B and D.

These are some cereals used for breakfast cereals.

Wheat used for Weetabix   ***Maize used for Cornflakes***   ***Oats used for porridge***   ***Rice used for Rice Krispies***

Design your own muesli

Work in teams and design your own recipe for muesli. Make a muesli with lots of crunch, flavour and a range of ingredients to add sweetness and colour.

You need a collection of cereal flakes, some dried fruits and nuts and seeds. Add sugar if needed.

To 'taste test' your muesli, serve it with some milk or yogurt and ask people to give their views. Score the taste test for appearance, texture, taste and flavour.

Present your ideas and discuss how to improve your product. Find out about the ingredients used in shop-bought muesli to help with your recipe ideas. Carry out a nutritional analysis of your final idea.

Cereal flakes	Wheat, oats, barley, rice
Dried fruit	Raisins, sultanas, dates, cranberries
Nuts	Hazelnuts, almonds, brazil nuts, coconut
Seeds	Pumpkin, sunflower, sesame

Design a muesli from ingredients like these

@ Hotlinks

The Association of Cereal Food Manufacturers' Breakfast Cereal Information Service

Kellogg's

Further work

There are many types of breakfast cereals. Visit a supermarket or use the Internet and find ten examples of breakfast foods made from these cereals: wheat, maize, oats.

To do

Other types of cereal include rye, millet, sorghum, quinoa, barley and buckwheat. Do some research and find how each of these cereals is used, and where it is grown.

Questions

1 Why are cereals such an important food crop?

2 What are the main nutrients found in cereals?

3 Maize, wheat and rice are the most popular cereals that we eat. Make a list of three foods made from each of these cereals.

4 Why is it a good idea to start the day with breakfast? Describe a 'good' breakfast that you would like to eat on a) a weekday, b) the weekend. Give reasons for your choice.

Flour

Wheat grains are ground into flour. The different parts of the wheat are used to make white, brown and wholemeal flour.

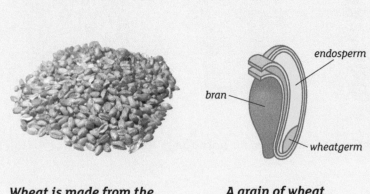

Wheat is made from the wheat grain.

A grain of wheat

Endosperm is the main part of the wheat grain which is milled to make flour.

Bran is the outer coating of the wheat grain which provides fibre and B vitamins.

Wheatgerm is the part of the wheat that grows into the new plant. It contains fat and B vitamins.

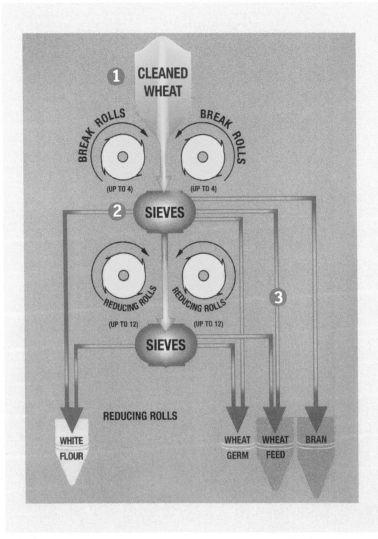

Making flour

1. Cleaned wheat is passed through rollers to break it into pieces to make semolina.

2. The wheat is sieved and the semolina is passed through more rollers to make fine flour.

3. Bran and wheatgerm separate out. These can be added back to white flour to make wholemeal flour.

4. All white and brown flours are fortified with minerals and vitamins.

What is the nutritional value of flour?

Flour contains starch and a little protein. White and brown flours have added calcium, iron, and the B vitamins thiamin and niacin.

Whole grains provide plenty of fibre, so it is best to eat foods made from whole wheat such as bread and pasta.

Flour in cookery

Flour is used to make:

- bread and cakes
- biscuits and sauces
- pasta and noodles.

It provides the bread, cakes and biscuits with their structure, and thickens sauces.

Gluten

Gluten is a form of protein found in wheat, rye, barley and oats. Gluten gives the structure for bread and cakes. Some people have an intolerance of gluten and buy gluten-free products. Here are some examples of gluten-free flours. They are made from cereals and legumes which don't contain gluten.

Gluten-free flour

Rice flour made from ground rice

To do

Make a list of 20 food products which are made from wheat. Find foods which use whole wheat and provide extra fibre.

Wheat allergy

True wheat allergy is extremely rare, but the number of people who believe they may suffer from food intolerance is rising. Wheat-based foods normally contain a mixture of ingredients, any of which could cause an adverse reaction.

Hotlinks

The Grain Chain – cereal growers' and bakers' education programme

Flour Advisory Bureau

Wright's home baking

Doves Farm Foods

Gram flour made from ground chickpeas

White bread flour – made from a blend of rice, potato, tapioca, maize and buckwheat

Questions

1 Name the different parts of the wheat grain and explain how they are used in flour making.

2 How is wheat milled into flour?

3 What is the nutritional value of flour, and what nutrients are added to white and brown flour?

4 What is gluten and how is it used in baking?

5 What ingredients are used to make gluten-free flours?

Baking with flour

When baking with flour, gluten and raising agents are important factors. Try these experiments to discover just how flour works.

Gluten

The gluten in flour helps to give bread, cakes and biscuits their structure.

 Experiment 1

Find out how much gluten is in different types of flour.

You will need:

- different types of flour – bread flour, plain flour, sauce flour, gluten-free flour, cornflour
- bowls, spoons, sieve, scales, baking tray

- Mix 100g of each flour with 50ml cold water to make a stiff ball of dough. Make sure you work in all the flour in the dough ball. Put in a bowl.
- Pour over some cold water and leave the dough ball for 30 minutes.
- Hold the dough ball in your hands and run the ball under the cold water tap to wash the dough. Work with your fingers until the water runs clear and is no longer milky. Hold a sieve under the ball to catch any bits of dough.
- You should be left with a gluten ball which looks like a piece of beige chewing gum.
- Weigh the ball and compare your result with the other flours.
- Bake the gluten ball in a hot oven (200°C/Gas 6) for 20 minutes and see how it has puffed up. The gluten is what gives the dough its structure.

A gluten ball

How much gluten is in different types of flour?

Tip: Bread flour has the most gluten, which helps give the bread its structure in order to rise.

Raising agents are needed for bread, cakes, scones and biscuits

Raising agents

Raising agents help to make bread, cakes, scones and biscuits rise so that they are not flat and hard.

Different raising agents include:

- yeast, used for bread and pizza
- baking powder, used for cakes and biscuits.

Self-raising flour has a raising agent added to it.

The raising agent in the flour reacts during cooking to produce carbon dioxide gas, and the mixture expands to give a light and airy texture.

Yeast as a raising agent

Yeast is a type of fungus which is a raising agent used to make breads and pizzas. It needs warmth, food and liquid, and time to grow, so when you make a bread dough, it must be warm. The flour provides the food and the water is the liquid.

Yeast is the raising agent for bread

 Experiment 2

Find the difference between plain and self-raising flour.

You will need:

- plain and self-raising flours
- 2 bowls, spoons, non-stick frying pan

- Mix 2 tablespoons of plain flour in a bowl with enough water to make a very soft mixture.
- Heat the frying pan and put the mixture in the pan. Cook like a pancake until firm, then turn over and cook the other side.
- Repeat with the self-raising flour. Notice how the self-raising flour mixture has lots of bubbles as it cooks.
- Compare the pancakes. Which one do you like best, and why? How did the raising agent change the mixture?

Questions

1 What is gluten and where is it found? Why is gluten important in bread-making?

2 What is a raising agent? List three raising agents and describe how they are used in baking.

3 How does a raising agent make a mixture rise?

4 List three recipes which use baking powder as a raising agent.

Bread

In the UK, we eat more than 9 million loaves of bread every day, and there are over 200 different varieties. Bread is an important source of carbohydrate, fibre, iron, calcium and thiamin.

Types of bread

The main types of bread are:

- **white bread** – made from flour which contains only the endosperm – the middle part of the grain
- **brown bread** – made from flour which has some bran and wheatgerm removed
- **wholemeal bread** – made from the whole wheat grain.

Some bread facts

- Most people eat bread at least once a day.
- Men eat bread more often than women.
- Each household buys on average 66 loaves a year.
- White sliced bread is the most popular.

There are many different bread recipes, shapes and sizes.

Here are some popular breads used for snacks, sandwiches and served with meals.

less than once a month 0.2%
less than once a week more than once a month 0.9%
once or twice a week 7.7%
very rarely or never 1.7%
twice a day 34.5%
3-6 times a week 15.4%
once a day 39.5%

Frequency of bread consumption

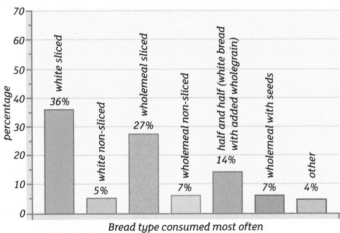

percentage

white sliced 36%
white non-sliced 5%
wholemeal sliced 27%
wholemeal non-sliced 7%
half and half (white bread with added wholegrain) 14%
wholemeal with seeds 7%
other 4%

Bread type consumed most often

The nation's daily bread

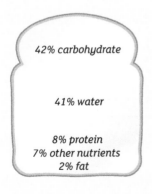

42% carbohydrate

41% water

8% protein
7% other nutrients
2% fat

The nutrients in bread

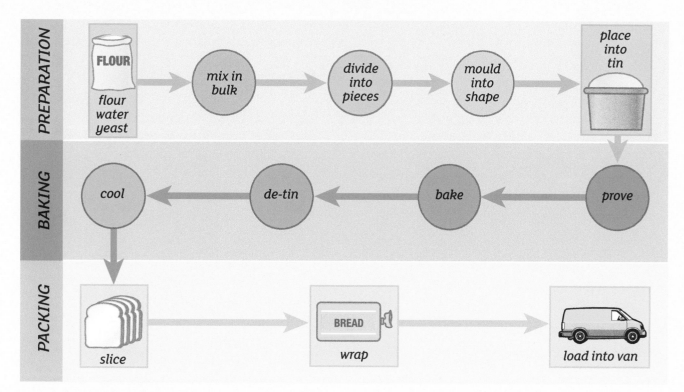

A day in the life of a loaf

Bread in a bakery

The ingredients (flour, water, salt and yeast) are mixed, then divided and shaped, put in a tin, proved and baked. Then the bread is cooled, sliced and wrapped.

Try making your own bread rolls.

Ingredients

300g strong bread flour
5g sugar
5g fast-action dried yeast
pinch of salt
200ml warm water
milk to glaze

Method

• Heat the oven to 220°C/ gas mark 7. Place greaseproof paper onto a baking tray.

• Sieve the flour and salt into a mixing bowl. Stir in the yeast and sugar.

• Add the warm water, and mix to a dough.

• Knead the dough for 5 minutes. Divide the dough into six pieces and shape into rolls.

• Place the rolls on the baking tray.

• Cover the dough with cling wrap and leave in a warm place for 30 minutes to allow it to rest and double in size.

• Brush the tops of the rolls with milk. Bake in the oven for 10–15 minutes until golden brown.

• Remove the rolls from the oven and cool.

 Hotlinks

Warburtons bakeries
The Federation of Bakers

Questions

1 What nutrients does bread provide?

2 Look at the charts on bread consumption. Describe in your own words a) how often we eat bread, b) which are the most popular breads.

3 What types of bread would you eat a) as snacks, b) with meals, c) as sandwiches? Give your reasons.

4 How is bread made in a factory? What do you think is the difference between factory- and home-made bread?

Pasta

Pasta is made from durum wheat, which is a high-protein wheat. It makes pasta that doesn't stick together when cooked.

Pasta is a food that contains starch, a carbohydrate which provides energy for our bodies. Starch is a complex carbohydrate, providing a slower release of energy than simple carbohydrates such as sugars. Pasta, especially wholemeal pasta, is a source of fibre.

How is pasta made?

- Durum wheat is ground into semolina.
- Water is added to make a dough.
- Dough is extruded through holes to make pasta shapes.
- The pasta is then dried and packed.

The type and shape of the holes control the finished shape of the pasta.

Types of pasta

There are over 200 different shapes of pasta.

- Long pasta: spaghetti, short spaghetti, fettucine (small ribbons)
- Short pasta: penne, farfalle (butterflies), fusilli (spirals)

Penne

Spaghetti

Fettucine

Fusilli

Farfalle

Different flavours

- Green – flavoured with spinach
- Red – flavoured with tomato
- Brown – made with mushrooms
- Black – coloured with squid ink

Cooking pasta is easy. Boil some water, add the pasta, cook to instructions, taste to see if it is *al dente* – chewy but firm to the bite – and drain.

Pasta comes in many different colours and shapes

The Pot Noodle range

To do

Invent a new flavour for Pot Noodle – you need some dried noodles and ingredients of your choice. Prepare the noodles with some fried vegetables and seasoning and test out your ideas with a tasting panel.

Hotlinks

Pasta Foods – the UK's leading dry pasta producer

Unilever – maker of Pot Noodle (search for 'Pot Noodle')

Pot noodle

Noodles have been eaten in China and throughout Asia for thousands of years, but the product Pot Noodle was invented in 1977. The UK factory makes 155 million pots a year. All you need for preparation is water, a kettle and a fork. Chicken-and-mushroom is the most popular flavour.

Questions

1 Pasta is used in many famous dishes. Write down as many as you can think of. Use a recipe book to help.

2 What type of wheat is used in pasta, and why is it chosen?

3 How is pasta made into different shapes?

4 How should pasta be cooked?

5 Give your views on Pot Noodle as the basis for a meal.

Maize

Maize, or corn, is an important grain that is used all over the world.

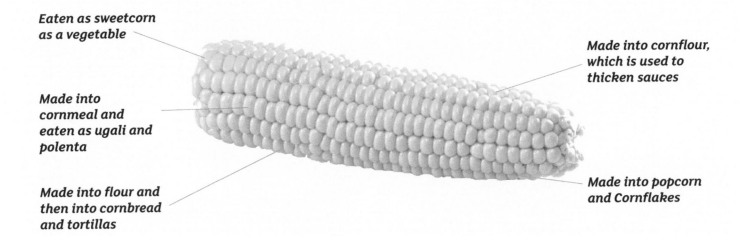

Eaten as sweetcorn as a vegetable

Made into cornmeal and eaten as ugali and polenta

Made into flour and then into cornbread and tortillas

Made into cornflour, which is used to thicken sauces

Made into popcorn and Cornflakes

Maize is made into many things

Maize first came from Mexico, and was taken to the Caribbean and then to Spain, the Middle East, Africa and China. All these countries have famous dishes that are made from maize.

Originally maize came in many colours and today, different varieties are used for cooking or feeding animals.

The picture opposite shows the maize seed.

- Endosperm – the starch is used for flour.
- The germ is used for corn oil.
- The outside husk is used for animal feed.

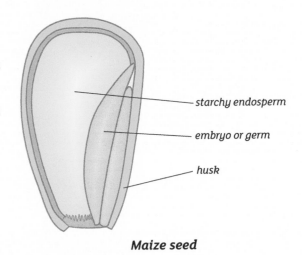

starchy endosperm

embryo or germ

husk

Maize seed

Popcorn

The popcorn that you eat in cinemas is made from a special type of maize which, when heated, explodes from the seed and puffs up.

Why does popcorn pop?

Each popcorn seed contains starch, water and oil. As the seed heats up, the water and oil heat up inside and the water becomes pressurised steam. The starch softens and the seed explodes with the pressure. The starch inside expands into a foam and sets to form popcorn.

 Hotlinks

The Popcorn Board site

Make your own popcorn

You need: Saucepan with lid, oil and popping corn

- Heat a little oil in a large saucepan.
- Add a layer of uncooked popcorn to cover the base of the pan.
- Put on the lid and shake the pan to cover the grains with oil.
- Leave on a medium heat and you will hear the grains popping. Do not take off the lid.
- When the popping is coming to an end, shake the pan and leave off the heat for two minutes.
- Open the lid and you should have a saucepan full of popcorn.
- Serve it with salt, spices or make a toffee sauce.

Cornflour

How does cornflour thicken a mixture?

Cornflour is used to thicken many ready-made products, such as tomato ketchup, chicken soup, lemon mousse, cheese spread, gravy, and custard.

Try this experiment. You need: Saucepan, bowl, wooden spoon, cornflour, milk

1 Mix the cornflour with a little milk in a bowl.

2 Heat the remaining milk in a saucepan and pour in the cornflour mixture.

3 Stir until thick. Watch what happens.

4 Flavour with salt and pepper, or sweeten with sugar and taste.

Cornflour is used to thicken many products

Genetically modified (GM) foods

The most common plants which have been modified are soya beans, maize and wheat. GM foods may have the DNA from one organism inserted into another to improve crop yields and reduce the need for chemical fertilisers.

Some people may not want to buy or eat genetically modified (GM) foods. In the EU, a food label shows if a food contains genetically modified organisms (GMOs), or contains ingredients produced from GMOs.

Ingredients

Tomato and herb sauce contains: tomato with acidity regulator: citric acid, tomato purée, water, sugar, cornflour, oregano, garlic purée, black pepper.
Genetically modified soyabean, salt, sugar, preservatives: sodium nitrite, antioxidant: sodium ascorbate.

How to store and cook

A food label must show if genetically modified foods are used

To do

Find 20 dishes from around the world that are made from maize. Describe how they are prepared and eaten.

Further work

Find out more about GM foods. Should GM crops be allowed? Give your views.

Questions

1 Name five foods which use maize as the main ingredient.

2 Which part of the maize seed is used for a) flour, b) oil?

3 Why does popcorn pop?

4 Name five products for sale in the shops which use cornflour (maize flour).

5 What is meant by GM?

The Chinese word for *food* is the same as their word for *rice*.
For half the people of the world, rice is their main food.

The importance of rice

Rice is gluten free so can be eaten by people who are allergic to gluten. Rice provides carbohydrates which are the fuel for the body, and a little protein, as well as minerals and vitamins.

There are many types of rice.

- **Long-grain rice:** The husk and bran layer are removed to make a white, polished grain. It is used especially for Chinese cooking.

- **Easy-cook rice** is steamed under pressure before it is milled to remove the husk. This rice cooks more quickly than other rice.

- **Brown long-grain rice** takes longer to cook, and is brown and chewy. Brown rice contains the bran so has more fibre, minerals and vitamins than ordinary rice.

Basmati rice is grown mainly in the foothills of the Himalayas in India and Pakistan. It has a wonderful flavour and aroma when cooked. It produces delicious, fluffy rice and is used to make Indian specialities such as pilaf or pilau rice.

Jasmine rice is also known as Thai fragrant rice and comes from Thailand. It has a sticky texture when cooked.

Short-grain rice is called pudding rice and the plump grains are used for milk puddings.

Arborio risotto rice makes the Italian dish risotto. When it cooks it is smooth and creamy, and yet it stays chewy.

Cooking rice

The cooking time for rice depends on the shape and variety of the grains.

There are many ways to boil rice. You can cook it in plenty of boiling water for 11 minutes then strain it.

How do people cook rice?

Work in groups and find out how people prepare and cook long-grain rice. Compare your findings with others.

Green cooking: Boil the water and add the rice. Bring the pot back to the boil then put on the lid and turn off the heat. You should find the rice has cooked in 11 minutes, and you have saved energy.

Basmati

Short grain

Arborio

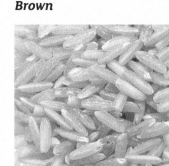
Brown

Easy cook

Long grain

Red rice

Wild rice

Many different types of rice are available

 Egg fried rice

Serves 4

Ingredients

100g easy-cook rice

3 tablespoons vegetable oil

2 eggs, beaten

1 clove garlic, crushed

100g frozen peas

1 carrot, peeled and grated

4 spring onions, chopped

4 tablespoons oyster sauce

2 tablespoons soy sauce

Method

• Cook the rice in boiling water according to packet instructions.

• Put the oil in a wok or frying pan and heat gently.

• Add the egg and stir, then stir in the garlic and the cooked rice.

• Cook and stir until the mixture is hot.

• Add the vegetables – the peas, carrots and spring onions, and stir.

• Now add the oyster and soy sauce and stir.

• Serve.

Is it Basmati rice?

True Basmati rice comes from specific regions, and the country of origin must be shown on the label.

But people have been claiming that other, cheaper varieties of rice are Basmati. **DNA testing technology** can identify varieties of rice and discover whether the rice is Basmati. DNA testing is also useful to detect whether fish are the right species, whether food contains peanuts, and if genetically modified ingredients have been used. This helps prevent fraud, and leads to safer food products.

Afghanistan

BASMATI

Pakistan

Nepal

India

Basmati rice-growing areas

 Hotlinks

The Rice Association

Tilda – a leading supplier of rice

 Further work

Investigate how DNA testing is used for food products.

 To do

Find out more about different types of rice from around the world.

? Questions

1 Explain why rice is such an important world food.

2 What is the nutritional value of rice?

3 Name four types of rice and describe dishes that can be made from each rice.

4 Why is DNA testing used for food testing?

Cooking oils, margarine, and butter provide many of the fats in our diet. Oils and fats come from animal and plant sources.

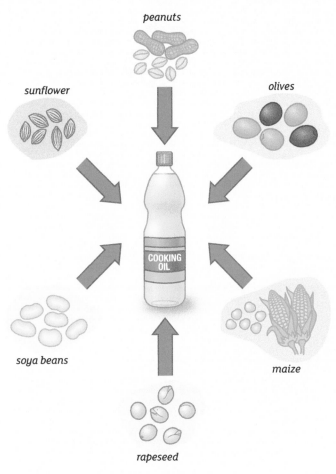

Sources of cooking oil

Cooking oils

Many plants provide us with cooking oil. The main types of oil are:

- sunflower oil – good for shallow frying and low in saturated fat
- peanut oil – sold as groundnut oil – reaches a high temperature for deep-fat frying
- corn oil – use in deep-fat frying
- rapeseed oil – good for frying
- soya bean oil – used in many food ingredients
- olive oil – delicious flavour, used in dressings.

Nutrition and fats

Most people need to cut down on the amount of fat they eat and try to replace saturated fat with unsaturated fat.

Fats which are high in saturated fat include butter, ghee and lard, coconut oil, coconut cream and palm oil.

Trans fats can be formed when liquid vegetable oils are turned into solid fats through the process of hydrogenation. Some margarines contain trans fats. We should avoid eating too many trans fats as they raise the type of cholesterol in the blood that causes heart disease.

This chart shows the percentage of saturated and unsaturated fat in cooking oils.

Type of oil	Saturated fat	Unsaturated fat	Cost for 1 litre
Corn oil	14%	81%	80p
Groundnut oil	20%	75%	£1.40
Rapeseed oil	7%	89%	£1
Sunflower oil	12%	84%	90p
Olive oil	14%	81%	£3.79

Vegetable oil is a blend of sunflower, safflower and groundnut oil. It has a bland taste and is cheaper than the pure oils.

Vegetable oils are liquid at room temperature. To use them in margarines and shortenings, they are hydrogenated – treated with hydrogen – to make them solid. The process adds hydrogen atoms to the chemical structure and makes the fat more saturated.

Margarine

Margarine was invented as a substitute for butter. Modern margarine is made from a mixture of animal and vegetable fats, and is less expensive than butter.

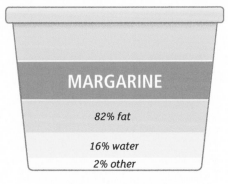

Nutrients in margarine

Many margarines are made by hydrogenating oil to make the fat harder, so check on the ingredients list for hydrogenated vegetable oil. Margarines can have added vitamin A and D to make them more nutritious.

Hard margarines are used in cooking and baking.

Healthier margarines are made from fats which are high in unsaturated fats.

Butter

Butter is made by churning cream.

Making butter

- The cream is separated from the milk.
- The cream is pasteurised to remove harmful bacteria.
- The cream is churned – the solids make butter and the buttermilk runs away for use as a food ingredient.
- The butter is moulded and packed – often salt is added.

A Tibetan woman churning milk by hand to make butter.

Making ghee

Ghee is a clarified butter used in Indian cooking. It will keep for 6–8 months without refrigeration.

To make ghee, melt butter in a saucepan until a white foam forms on the surface. Keep heating gently until the butter ghee is clear and golden and the foam has sunk to the bottom. When it is ready, it smells of buttered popcorn, so take off the heat, cool and strain into a jar.

Making ghee

To do

Find out more about sustainable farming of cooking oil by using the Internet.

Further work

Discover more about ten different kinds of oil used in cooking.

Questions

1 Which oil would you choose for a) use in frying; b) its flavour; c) its lower price?

2 Sort the cooking oils in the chart on the opposite page into order, with a) the highest in saturated fat first; b) the highest in unsaturated fat first.

3 Explain how the following foods are made: margarine, butter, ghee.

Milk is the first and most important food for young animals, and contains many valuable nutrients.

Nutrients in milk

Milk contains protein for growth and repair, carbohydrate for energy, and fat with fat-soluble vitamins including B vitamins. It is an excellent source of calcium and phosphorus – essential for the healthy growth and maintenance of teeth and bones.

Teenagers' diet low in calcium

A survey showed that 24% of girls aged 11–14 years old and 19% of girls aged 15–18 had calcium intakes below the recommended levels. Milk and dairy foods provide a rich source of vitamins and minerals essential to good health including calcium. The Dairy Council suggests we eat three portions of dairy foods each day. You could have a glass of milk at breakfast or milk on your cereal, a cheese sandwich at lunch and yogurt in the evening.

90% water

5% carbohydrate
3% protein
2% other
2% fat

Nutrients in semi-skimmed milk

Calcium needs	Foods to eat
Boys 11–18 1000mg calcium a day	250ml semi-skimmed milk, 200g pot of yogurt, 45g low-fat cheese. These portions provide approximately 1000mg of calcium.
Girls 11–18 800mg calcium a day	200ml semi-skimmed milk, 200g pot of yogurt, 30g low fat cheese. These portions provide approximately 842mg of calcium

Type of milk	Fat content	Facts
Whole milk	2%	
Semi-skimmed milk	1.7%	Most popular type of milk in the UK.
Skimmed milk	0.2%	Slightly more watery than other types of milk.
Organic milk	Nutrition content the same as other types of milk	From cows that have been grazed on pasture that has used no chemical fertilisers or pesticides.
Jersey and Guernsey milk	Higher in fat and fat-soluble vitamins than other types of milk	Milk from Jersey or Guernsey breeds of cow with a rich and creamy taste.
Sterilised milk	Available whole, semi-skimmed and skimmed	Heat treated to destroy nearly all the bacteria.
Evaporated milk	9.4%	Has a cooked flavour and golden colour. A concentrated, sterilised milk – twice as concentrated as ordinary milk. Sold in cans.
Condensed milk	10.10%	Concentrated in the same way as evaporated milk, but with added sugar. Sold in cans.
Dried milk powder	0.6% fat – water added to mix	Made by drying the water from milk.

Making milk safe to drink

Most milk is pasteurised – the milk is heated to kill harmful micro-organisms such as bacteria, yeasts and moulds. A lot of milk is homogenised – a process which breaks down the fat globules in milk so there is no cream on the top.

Milk and cream

Cream is the high fat layer that floats to the top of untreated milk. Cream is made into many foods such as soups, sauces and ice cream.

There are lots of types of cream:

Single cream: 18% fat	Double cream: 48% fat
Whipping cream: 38% fat	Clotted cream (solid cream): 55% fat

Different types of milk

Cows produce milk

Hotlinks

The Dairy Council

Waitrose – search for 'milk'

To do

1 Plan a day's diet to include three different dairy foods.

2 Some people do not drink milk or eat dairy products. What foods could they eat to provide calcium?

Further work

1 Carry out a taste test on the different types of milk. Here are some descriptors you can use: creamy, watery, milky, tasteless, sweet, greasy.

2 Find some recipes which use the different types of cream.

Questions

1 What nutrients are found in milk?

2 Why are milk and milk products useful foods for teenagers?

3 How would you encourage teenagers to drink more milk?

4 How is milk made safe to drink?

5 Make a list of the types of milk, starting with the one with the highest fat content.

6 Why do you think people want to use sterilised, evaporated and dried milk?

7 How is cream made?

Yogurt and ice cream

Cow's milk is the most common milk used for yogurt, but it is also made from the milk of sheep, goats and buffalo. Yogurt is milk which has been fermented by adding bacteria.

How yogurt is made

- Cows produce milk on the farm
- The milk arrives at the dairy from the farm in refrigerated lorries.
- The milk is homogenised to mix up the milk and cream, then pasteurised to make it safe. The milk is cooled.
- A starter culture of special bacteria is added and the mixture is held at 40°C for several hours to make yogurt. The process is controlled by computer.
- When ready, it is cooled to stop the bacteria working. Fruit and flavours are added.
- The yogurt is filled into pots, coded and lidded, then packaged and chilled to 5°C for sale.

The whole process takes about 22 hours.

Making yogurt in a factory

 Make your own yogurt

Many people make their own yogurt at home. Some families have a starter culture which has been used in the family for years.

- For safety, make sure all the equipment is clean and the yogurt is kept covered.
- Heat 500ml of milk to 70°C – test with a food probe.
- Cover and cool the milk to 43°C.
- Add one tablespoon of fresh, plain yogurt and pour into a thermos flask or leave covered in a warm place.
- Leave for 8 hours to thicken.
- Cool, and keep in the refrigerator.

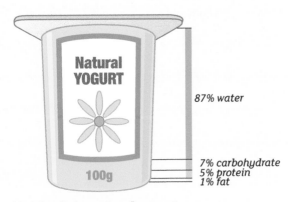

Nutrients in natural yogurt

87% water
7% carbohydrate
5% protein
1% fat
100g

Types of yogurt

- **Live yogurt** has been fermented with live bacteria. It has a smooth, creamy texture and a fresh, slightly tangy flavour.
- **Bio yogurt** has added 'friendly bacteria' to help our digestive system stay healthy.
- **Greek yogurt** can be made from cow or ewe milk. It has been strained, which makes it thick, mild and creamy.
- **Set yogurt** is set in its pot and is thick.
- **Whole-milk yogurt** is made from whole milk, and **low-fat yogurt** is made from skimmed milk.
- **Drinking yogurt** has a pouring texture suitable for drinks.

Cream Vanilla

Milk Sugar

The ingredients are mixed together

The ice cream is then pasteurised by machine

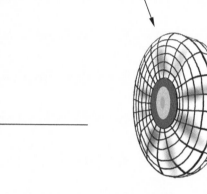

Air is added to the mixture

Ice cream production in a factory

Ice cream

To make vanilla ice cream, milk, cream and sugar are mixed with vanilla for flavour.

The mixture is pasteurised, then cooled to 4°C and crystallised in tanks.

Air is added to make the ice cream smooth.

The mixture passes through a freezer barrel and at the end the mix is -4°C and still quite soft. The mixture is beaten and fluffed.

The ice cream is put into tubs, packed and passed into a freezer tunnel at -24°C.

It is now ready for distribution to the shops.

Hotlinks

Ben & Jerry's – leading ice cream manufacturer

Rachel's Organic – leading yogurt manufacturer

Further work

Find out more about the health claims for bio yogurts.

To do

Invent your own flavour of ice cream – you can get ideas from the Internet. Explain why you have chosen the flavour.

Questions

1 What types of animal milk can be used for yogurt?

2 How is yogurt made?

3 What different types of yogurt are available for sale?

4 Create a sweet or savoury dish using yogurt as part of the recipe. Describe how it is made.

5 How is ice cream made? Why is it important to keep the equipment completely clean when making yogurt and ice cream?

Cheese is usually made from cow's milk, but the milk from sheep, goats, buffalo and yaks can be used too. It takes 10 litres of milk to make 1kg of cheese.

Cheddar cheese

Cheddar is the UK's favourite cheese, with 55% of all cheese sales. The next most popular cheese is Mozzarella. Cheddar is named after the Cheddar Gorge caves in Somerset where the cheese used to be stored to ripen.

Cheese nutrition

Cheese is a nutritious food, as it contains:

- protein: essential for growth
- vitamin A: important for the immune system, bone growth, vision and cell division
- vitamin B12: needed for maintaining healthy red blood cells and nerve cells
- calcium: vital for the formation and maintenance of strong bones and teeth
- vitamin D: needed to help the absorption of calcium.

Most cheese contains about 35% fat. You can buy reduced-fat cheeses with less fat.

How is cheese made?

The milk is pasteurised and a starter is added which turns the milk sour.

Rennet is added to clot the milk and separate it into curds (solids) and whey (liquid).

The curd is cut and the whey drains away.

The lumps of curd are washed to remove more whey.

Salt is added to flavour and preserve the cheese.

The cheese is pressed into moulds and pressed to remove more whey.

It is left to ripen to develop taste and texture – strong cheese takes longer to mature and costs more to buy. The cheese is packed ready for sale.

Nearly all cheese sold or produced in the UK is made from non-animal rennet, so can be eaten by vegetarians.

Cheese-making

Cows are milked

Milk is collected by tankers

Milk is pasteurised in large steel drums

Curd and whey form and are then separated

Whey is drained and the cheese pressed in moulds

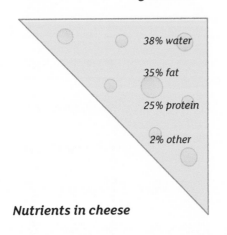

38% water
35% fat
25% protein
2% other

Nutrients in cheese

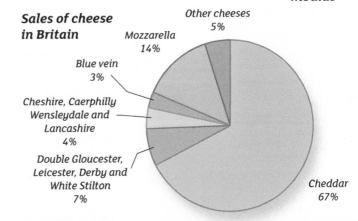

Sales of cheese in Britain

Other cheeses 5%
Mozzarella 14%
Blue vein 3%
Cheshire, Caerphilly Wensleydale and Lancashire 4%
Double Gloucester, Leicester, Derby and White Stilton 7%
Cheddar 67%

Cheese is made from the milk of different animals

Paneer

Paneer is a cheese which comes from north India. It contains no rennet, so is suitable for vegetarians. It is made by adding an acid food, such as lemon juice or vinegar, to hot milk. The acid separates the curds from the whey, and the excess liquid is drained off. The curds are lightly pressed into a block and the paneer is chilled. Mutter Paneer is the famous curry of paneer and peas from the Punjab.

Paneer is a cheese used in cooking

Cottage cheese

Cottage cheese is a cheese curd product with a mild flavour. It is drained, but not pressed, so some whey remains. It is low in fat and used in salads.

Further work

Carry out some research to find the differences between some of the cheeses shown on these pages, and the difference between hard and soft cheese.

Fromage frais

This is a popular food with children and is made in a similar way to cheese. Rennet and a starter culture are added to the milk. The curds are then stirred, which gives fromage frais the same texture as yogurt. Fruit is often added for flavour.

Fromage frais is a soft cheese like yogurt

Hotlinks

cheese.com – all about cheese

To do

Write your own poem about cheese.

Questions

1 What types of milk can be used to make cheese?

2 What nutrients are found in cheese, and what is their function?

3 Explain how cheese is made.

4 List the five most popular cheeses in the UK.

5 How are these three foods made and used: a) paneer; b) cottage cheese, c) fromage frais?

Meat comes from animals: Beef comes from beef cattle, lamb comes from young sheep, and pork, bacon and ham come from pigs.

Sources of meat

Beef cattle live outdoors for most of the year and graze on grass.

Lamb comes from sheep that have been reared outdoors and fed on grass, or on hay if grass is in short supply. We get fresh British lamb from June; lamb comes from New Zealand in the winter.

Meat that is certified Halal has been slaughtered in accordance with Islamic law. New Zealand is the world's largest exporter of Halal-slaughtered sheepmeat.

Pigs can be farmed intensively in indoor pens or outdoors in a free range system.

Meat and nutrition

Meat is a good source of protein, which is needed by the body for growth and repair. Nowadays, meat is produced with less fat, and often the fat is removed when it is prepared for sale. Fat gives flavour to meat when it is cooked, especially roast and grilled meat.

Red meats such as beef and lamb are a good source of easily absorbed iron, which we need for healthy blood.

To reduce the fat in meat:

- buy the leanest red meat, so that there is less waste
- cut visible fat from the meat before cooking
- dry-fry meat such as bacon – without adding any fat
- grill, bake or microwave without adding fat to meat.

Buying and cooking meat

- Raw meat contains bacteria, so great care is needed during preparation and cooking.
- Cover and store raw foods such as meat separately in the lower part of the refrigerator.
- Keep a separate chopping board to prepare raw meats, to avoid cross-contamination with other foods.
- Wash your hands after handling meat to avoid contaminating other foods.
- Defrost frozen meats thoroughly (unless otherwise stated on the packaging) and do not re-freeze once thawed.
- Make sure burgers and sausages are thoroughly cooked and piping hot before serving.

Different types of meat

You can reduce the fat and saturated fat in a burger by choosing different types of meat.

This chart shows the nutritional values in 100 grams of meat.

	Energy kcal	Fat g	Protein g	Iron mg
Beef mince, raw	225	16.2	19.7	1.4
Beef mince, extra lean, raw	174	9.6	21.9	1.5
Pork mince, raw	164	9.7	19.2	0.9
Lamb mince, raw	196	13.3	19.1	1.6
Chicken mince, raw	106	1.1	24	0.5
Turkey mince, raw	105	1.6	22.6	0.6

A burger-making machine

@ Hotlinks

Meat Matters – website created by meat producers

Meat and Education – educational website about meat

To do

Find out more about the cuts of meat for beef, pork and lamb and explain how they are cooked and made into famous dishes.

Make a lower-fat burger

Buy lower-fat minced meat – it could be chicken, turkey, pork, lamb or beef.

Ingredients:

250g minced meat – beef, pork, lamb, turkey or chicken
½ small onion, very finely chopped
salt and pepper
egg to bind
a little oil for frying
burger buns, sliced tomato, lettuce to serve

Method:

- Mix together the minced meat, chopped onion, salt and pepper and enough egg to stick the mixture together.
- Pat into burgers, or use a burger maker. Make sure the burgers are all the same size.
- Fry or grill for 10 minutes on each side until thoroughly cooked.
- Serve in a lightly toasted bun with some salad.

48% water

27% protein

25% fat

Nutrition in a burger patty

? Questions

1. List the three types of animal used for meat and the names of meat they produce.
2. What is the nutritional value of red meat?
3. How can you lower the amount of fat when buying and cooking meat?
4. How should meat be stored and handled for safety?
5. Compare the nutritional value of burgers made from different meats. Which two do you think are the healthiest? Give your reasons.

Nearly 40% of all the meat we eat is chicken, and it is a nutritious food that can be cooked in many ways.

Chicken and nutrition

Chicken is lower in fat and higher in protein than red meat, and contains vitamins B6 and B12 and selenium – an antioxidant that helps the body fight against cancer.

This table compares the energy, fat and protein in chicken.

Raw (100g)	Energy (kcal)	Fat (g)	Protein (g)
Chicken skinless, light meat	106	1.1	24
Chicken meat and skin	201	4	19.1

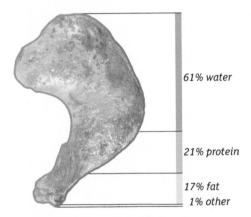

61% water

21% protein

17% fat
1% other

Nutrition in a roast chicken leg

Jamie Oliver

How are chickens farmed?

860 million chickens are reared for food in the UK each year, but 95% of chickens are reared indoors with no daylight and little room to move about. Celebrity chef Jamie Oliver campaigned for chickens to be reared in better conditions with natural daylight and room to roam.

However, if chickens have more space and are slower growing, the chicken will cost more to buy.

The different types of chicken you can buy in the shops are described below.

Standard chickens

Chickens are kept indoors with no natural daylight and grow to about 2 kilos in weight in five weeks. These fast-growing chickens have long periods of artificial light each day to make them eat more and grow more quickly. Each chicken has a space the size of an A4 sheet of paper. Birds are 39–42 days old when they are slaughtered.

Freedom Food

The RSPCA welfare standards, amongst other things, limit how fast the chickens can be grown, to reduce the chance of the birds injuring their legs or having heart problems. Barn-reared chickens are kept indoors all the time but have a bit more room (15 birds per square metre), space to perch and bales of hay to peck.

FREEDOM FOOD
RSPCA MONITORED

Certification Mark

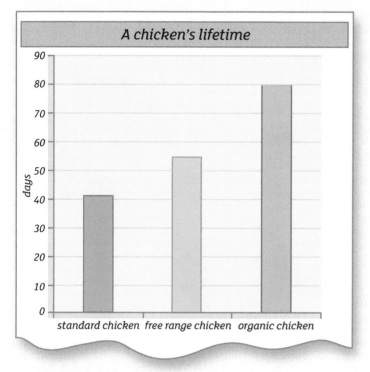

A chicken's lifetime

How long do farmed chickens live?

Do not let raw chicken drip onto other foods

Free-range chicken

These chickens are allowed outside in the woods and fields and have more room to move about. They are reared in large sheds. Birds are 56 days old when they are slaughtered.

Organic chicken

These are reared in small flocks, roam about in fields and peck for food. They are given organic food to eat. Birds are 80 days old when they are slaughtered. Organic birds are three times as expensive as standard chickens.

@ Hotlinks

Great British Chicken – website about British chicken

Support Chicken Now – RSPCA and Freedom Food website about chicken

To do

Carry out some research to find out about the different ways of farming chicken. Use the Internet to find information. Compare the cost of chickens and chicken portions.

Present your ideas to show which method of farming you prefer – but consider the cost of rearing and the selling price of the chicken.

Storing and using chicken

- Raw and cooked chicken should be stored separately.
- Never leave cooked chicken at room temperature for more than two hours. If not eaten immediately, cooked chicken should be kept hot or refrigerated.
- Fresh or frozen chicken should be put away in the fridge or freezer immediately on getting home.
- After preparing raw chicken, wash hands, all equipment and work surfaces, to stop cross-contamination to other foods.

Questions

1 What nutrients can be found in chicken? When you remove the skin, how does the nutrition change?

2 Explain why it is cheaper to farm standard chickens compared with free-range and organic chicken. Which type of chicken would you prefer to buy? Give your reasons.

3 Make a list of rules for storing and using raw chicken.

Experts say we should eat at least two portions of fish a week, one of which should be oil-rich. Fish is low in calories, and high in protein.

Fish, crustaceans and molluscs

Oily fish

Oily fish supplies Vitamins A and D and omega 3 fatty acids, which are important for a healthy heart, lowering cholesterol levels and general health.

The main oil-rich fish are salmon, trout, mackerel, sardines, and herring – fresh, frozen or canned. Tuna is only counted as an oily fish if it is fresh or frozen.

DID YOU KNOW...

We choose Alaskan Pollock for these Fish Fingers because it's a natural source of **Omega 3**. **Omega 3** plays an important part in the diet, helping to maintain a healthy heart and contributing to brain development. Fish Finger Megas are the ideal way to give your kids **Omega 3** without them knowing as part of a varied and balanced diet and healthy lifestyle.

Birds Eye

100% fillet fish fingers.

*Guideline Daily Amounts are guidelines only for 5-10 year olds. Individual requirements will vary

Nutrition Information Typical Values	Per 2 mega fish fingers (110g) grilled
Energy - kJ	
- kcal Calories	

Fish are a good source of omega 3

Fish and chips

Fish and chips is a famous British takeaway meal of deep-fried, battered fish and potatoes. 250 million portions of fish and chips are sold in the UK each year and on Friday nights, 20% of the meals bought out of the home are from the fish and chip shop.

Cod is the most popular fish, but chip shops are changing to pollack due to overfishing of cod.

Types of food from the sea

Seafood can be divided into three separate categories:

1 **White fish** includes cod, haddock, plaice, whiting, pollack, coley, dover sole, dogfish, skates, rays.

2 **Oil-rich fish** includes herring, mackerel, sardines, whitebait, tuna.

3 **Shellfish** includes:

- molluscs – scallops, oysters, cockles, mussels, winkles
- crustacea – prawns, scampi, crabs, lobsters, shrimps octopus, squid, cuttlefish.

Fish stocks in decline

The amount of fish being caught around the world is decreasing each year. Fishing fleets use bigger vessels, better nets and new technology for spotting fish. The diets of 2.6 billion people around the world depend on fish.

One scientist says: 'Unless we change the way we manage all the ocean species, as working ecosystems, then this century is the last century of wild seafood.' Research shows that if the seas and stocks of fish could be well managed, fish stocks and the range of species would improve.

Birds Eye make fish fingers from cod and from pollack

Fish fingers

The first fish finger was produced in 1955, by its inventor Clarence Birdseye. Fish fingers are usually made from cod, but as North Sea supplies fall, manufacturers are beginning to use other types of fish such as pollack and hoki. Pollack is smaller than cod, with more muscle, and the flesh is moist.

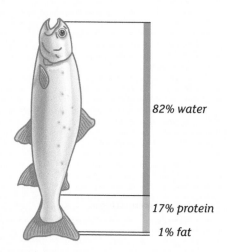

82% water

17% protein

1% fat

Nutrition of cod

@ Hotlinks

Birds Eye

The Sea Fish Industry Authority

Scottish Salmon Producers' Organisation

To do

Find out more about world fishing. What types of fish are being overfished? What can be done to help the future of wild fish as a food?

Birds Eye Omega 3 fish fingers are made from Alaskan pollack fillets, which are a rich source of omega 3. The company says that pollack is a more sustainable fish, and the cod catch will reduce by 2 million fish a year.

Taste test

Carry out a blind tasting. Prepare fish fingers made from cod and pollack. Serve both fish fingers at the same temperature. Do not tell people which fish is which. Find out which one they like best.

Salmon is a very popular fish, and with the success of fish farming, the price for salmon is going down. Fish farms are found in sheltered waters near the coastline and the fish are kept in large nets. Salmon is one of the major sources of omega 3 fatty acids.

Freshwater fish

Popular fish produced in fresh water include trout and salmon.

Carp is a freshwater fish popular with eastern Europeans, especially at Christmas time.

Fish farming

Questions

1 What is the nutritional value of fish?

2 What is omega 3 and why is it important in our diet?

3 Which is your favourite fish? Describe why you like it. How is it cooked, and what can you serve with it to make a meal?

A diet rich in a variety of fruits and vegetables can make us healthier. The aim is to eat at least five portions of fruit and vegetables each day.

150ml smoothie

2 tablespoons of chopped fresh or canned fruit

What is a '5 a day' serving?

2-3 satsumas

1 medium banana, apple or orange

Five a day

Fruit and vegetables are:

- packed with vitamins and minerals
- helpful in maintaining a healthy weight
- an excellent source of fibre and antioxidants
- known to reduce the risk of heart disease, stroke and some cancers.

For your five a day, fruit and vegetables can be fresh, frozen, dried or canned. One portion a day can be a fruit juice or smoothie.

1 tablespoon of dried apricots or raisins

How much?

A portion is about 80 grams of fruit:

- 2–3 small fruit such as satsumas
- 1 medium-sized fruit such as an apple, banana, orange
- 1 tablespoon of dried fruit such as apricots or raisins
- 150ml juice or smoothie.

You can count juices or smoothies only once a day because they contain very little fibre and are high in fruit sugars, which can cause tooth decay if taken often between meals.

5 A DAY

Just Eat More
(fruit & veg)

5 A DAY

The 5 A DAY logo on food packaging shows how many portions of fruit and vegetables a typical serving of the food contains. The logo on the right indicates one portion of fruit and vegetables.

Try eating a rainbow of coloured fruit each day. For example, red apples, orange satsumas, yellow banana, green grapes, blue blueberries, purple plums. The colours each provide different minerals and vitamins.

A rainbow of fruit

Case study: SuperJam™

Fraser Doherty first started selling jam door-to-door in Edinburgh when he was 14. He got the recipes from his grandmother and then adapted them by sweetening with grape juice instead of sugar, and using highly nutritious fruits such as blueberries and cranberries. The SuperJam™ range, with no-added-sugar 'super fruit' spreads, was born. Now the teenager, who persuaded Waitrose to sell his home-made jam, is on track to be running a £1 million business before he leaves university.

Fraser Doherty's SuperJam

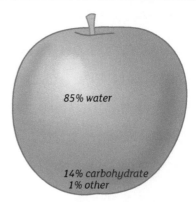

85% water

14% carbohydrate
1% other

Nutrition in a blueberry

Did you know?

- Blueberries are one of the very few blue foods on earth.

- 90% of the world's blueberries come from North America. Blueberries are harvested from mid-April until early October, with peak harvest in July, which is also known as National Blueberry Month.

- The Dorset Blueberry Company produces British-grown blueberries for farmers' markets and shops. Blueberries contain vitamin C, folic acid, and fibre.

Further work

Which fruits are in season in the UK at the moment? Research on the Internet or visit a supermarket to look at labels. Fill in a chart like the one below to show when fruits grow. We import many fruits from around the world.

Find out where 10 imported fruits are grown and do some research to discover their growing season when they are ready to eat.

January	February	March	April	May	June	July	August	September	October	November	December

@ Hotlinks

SuperJam

The National Health Service's 5-a-day site

To do

If you could create a fruit spread, what flavours would you choose and why? Describe how your spread could be used for meals and snacks.

Questions

1 Why are fruits a healthy food?

2 Make a list of different fruits you can buy a) fresh, b) frozen, c) dried, d) canned.

3 Keep a food diary of all your food and drinks for a day. Give yourself a mark out of 5 for the number of portions of fruit and vegetables you ate. Suggest ways you could improve – if necessary.

4 Draw a rainbow and label each section with fruits and vegetables for each colour. Compare your results with others.

Vegetables

Vegetables provide us with a range of nutrients. Root vegetables are a good source of carbohydrate; peas, beans and lentils provide protein; and all vegetables provide dietary fibre, which is essential for a healthy digestive system. Red, orange and yellow vegetables are good sources of vitamin A, and vitamin C is found in leafy vegetables such as salad greens.

What is a '5 a day' serving?

2 broccoli spears

1 medium tomato

7 cherry tomatoes

3 sticks of celery

4 cm piece of cucumber

3 heaped tablespoons of carrots, peas or sweetcorn

3 heaped tablespoons of baked beans

Five a day

The aim of the 5-a-day campaign is to eat at least five portions of fruit and vegetables each day. They can be fresh, frozen, dried or canned.

Portion sizes

Green vegetables:

- 2 broccoli spears, 8 cauliflower florets, 4 heaped tablespoons of green beans

Cooked vegetables:

- 3 heaped tablespoons of cooked vegetables such as carrots, peas or sweetcorn

Salad vegetables:

- 3 sticks of celery, 4cm of cucumber, 1 medium tomato, 7 cherry tomatoes

Canned and frozen vegetables:

- Use the same quantity as you would eat fresh. For example, 3 heaped tablespoons of canned or frozen carrots, peas or sweetcorn

Pulses and beans:

- 3 heaped tablespoons of baked beans, kidney beans, butter beans or chick peas. Beans and pulses do count in the five a day, but only as one of the five portions, no matter how much you eat.

Because they are considered a 'starchy' food, potatoes don't count towards your five a day.

Vegetables in season

Vegetables come from around the world and are available all year. But if we buy locally grown vegetables, in season, it helps to support local food producers and reduces the food miles that the products travel. In season, the price of vegetables is usually lower and the vegetables are fresher.

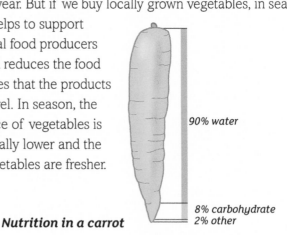

90% water

8% carbohydrate
2% other

Nutrition in a carrot

Preparing vegetables

Many vegetables can be eaten raw. Wash to remove any dirt, and peel if necessary. Peel thinly because nutrients are stored just below the skin.

Steaming is a nutritious way to cook vegetables, because the nutrients are not lost in the cooking water. Boil green vegetables in a little boiling water for a short time, and use the cooking water for sauce or gravy. Don't cook any vegetables for too long, as nutrients will be lost.

Vegetable groups

Fungi: mushrooms such as button, chestnut, flat, oyster

Roots and tubers: beetroot, carrots, cassava, parsnips, potatoes, radish, sweet potatoes, yams

Bulbs: garlic, leeks, onions, shallots, spring onions

Leafy greens and brassicas: Brussels sprouts, cabbage, pak choi, spinach

Flowers: broccoli, cauliflower

Stalks and shoots: asparagus, celery, globe artichokes, fennel

Squashes: courgettes, cucumbers, gourds, marrows, pumpkins, squashes

Vegetable fruits: aubergine, avocado, breadfruit, chillies, plantain, peppers, tomatoes

Pods and seeds: broad beans, French beans, okra, peas, sweetcorn

Fungi

Roots and tubers

Bulbs

Leafy greens and brassicas

Flowers

Stalks and shoots

Squashes

Vegetable fruits

Pods and seeds

 Hotlinks

Think Vegetables – information site provided by Mack Vegetables

The National Health Service's 5-a-day site

 Further work

Which vegetables are in season in the UK at the moment? Research on the Internet, ask people who grow vegetables, or visit a supermarket and look at labels. Fill in a chart like the one below to show when the vegetables grow. Create and test three recipes using some of the vegetables. Carry out a nutritional analysis for your recipe and make a food label.

January	February	March	April	May	June	July	August	September	October	November	December

 To do

Make a list of the nine vegetable groups. Add these vegetables to one of the groups:

Lettuce, lentils, okra, aubergine, turnips, rocket, purple sprouting broccoli, carrots, peas, courgettes, button mushrooms, leeks, watercress, tomatoes, cassava, avocado.

 Questions

1 Why are vegetables important for a healthy diet?

2 Plan four main meals with two portions of vegetables for each meal. Use fresh vegetables for two of the meals, and frozen, canned or dried vegetables for the other two. Give reasons for your choice.

3 How can you prepare and cook vegetables healthily?

Tomatoes are the most popular fruit/vegetable used in food products. They are found in many different forms, and are a source of important nutrients.

Varieties of tomatoes

Tomato facts

Look at all the forms of tomatoes you can buy:

Canned tomatoes, tomato sauce, tomato ketchup, toppings for pizza, passata used for pasta sauces, tomato salsa, tomato juice and sun-dried tomatoes.

The tomato originally came from South America, like potatoes, chillies and aubergines, but the Spanish took the plants around the world and they were grown in many countries from the 1600s.

Tomatoes come in many sizes and colours – cherry tomatoes are very small; beef tomatoes, which can be stuffed with rice and herbs, are large. Plum tomatoes are long instead of round, and are used for canned tomatoes.

Most tomatoes are red, but you can find yellow, orange and green ones in specialist shops. The first tomatoes were yellow, and were called golden apples.

Health claims

Tomatoes are a good source of vitamins A, C and E and antioxidants, particularly lycopene, a bright red pigment found in tomatoes and other red fruits. When tomatoes are cooked the lycopene is more available and so tomato purée, canned tomatoes and tomato ketchup are good sources of lycopene. Research has shown that lycopene may protect the body from heart disease and some cancers.

Fresh tomato salsa

Serves 4

Ingredients

15ml olive oil
1 clove garlic, peeled and sliced
½ small onion, finely chopped
½ green pepper, de-seeded and finely chopped
1 red chilli, de-seeded and finely chopped
500g tomatoes
Juice of ½ lemon
1 tbsp fresh coriander, finely chopped
1 tsp caster sugar
salt and black pepper

94% water

3% carbohydrate
3% other

Nutrition in a tomato

Method

• Heat the oil in a saucepan and gently fry the garlic, onion, green pepper and chilli for 10 minutes, until soft.

• Peel the tomatoes – put in a bowl of very hot water to soften the skin and peel off. Then chop finely and put in a bowl.

• Add the mixture from the saucepan, lemon juice, and coriander and stir. Season with sugar, salt and pepper.

• Leave to cool to allow the flavours to develop. Serve with bread, burgers and dips.

Tomato ketchup

Tomato ketchup is so popular that there is even a cook book with recipes using it.

Heinz invented its tomato ketchup in 1876, and today over 11 billion bottles are sold each year to over 140 countries around the world.

Ingredients in tomato ketchup

Tomato purée, sugar, spirit vinegar, tomato concentrate, salt, modified maize starch, flavouring.

- Why does the ketchup label say that 100g is made from 126g of tomatoes?

Because ketchup is made from cooked tomatoes and when they are cooked, tomatoes lose water so it takes 126g to make 100g of cooked tomatoes. This gives the ketchup its rich, strong tomato flavour.

Packaging ketchup

People use Heinz ketchup in many different ways and places. As a result, the company has invented lots of different packaging. There is reduced-sugar and reduced-salt tomato ketchup, and organic tomato ketchup.

Glass bottle

Upside-down plastic pot

Organic

Plastic 'squeeze-me' packaging

Hotlinks

Tomato Growers' Association

Heinz tomato ketchup

To do

Find famous tomato dishes from 20 countries around the world. Try to make one for others to taste.

Questions

1 Explain why you think the tomato is such an important food ingredient all around the world.

2 What is the nutritional value of the tomato?

3 How would you use tomato ketchup with meals and with cooking? Give five ideas.

4 What are the main ingredients in tomato ketchup?

5 Why do you think that ketchup is packed in so many different ways?

Potatoes and starchy vegetables

Potatoes are a staple food supplying us with energy from carbohydrate, fibre to help digestion, vitamins C and B6, and minerals such as potassium and magnesium.

Cooking potatoes

Potatoes can be served boiled, as mashed potato, chips, roast, jacket and wedges. Potatoes are an essential ingredient for many famous dishes from around the world:

- Aloo gobi – a spicy potato and cauliflower dish from the Punjab
- Gnocchi – small Italian dumplings made from potato flour
- Hash browns – American dish of slivers of potato fried until golden
- Polish kluski – dumplings with potato, egg and flour
- Rosti – a grated potato dish from Switzerland
- Bombay potatoes – Indian dish of spicy chunks of potato

The varieties of potatoes have different characteristics. The label on a bag of potatoes tells you how to cook each variety.

Key Potato Varieties

Charlotte Desiree Estima

King Edward Maris Peer Maris Piper

Key potato varieties

2008 Agriculture and Horticulture Development Board – Source: The Potato Council

Main potato varieties

Charlotte – yellow flesh, firm texture, used for salads.

Desiree – red skin and firm texture, used for boiling, baking, roasting and chips.

Estima – firm, moist texture, used for boiling, wedges and baking.

King Edward – creamy flesh, flour texture, used for roasting and chips.

Maris Peer – creamy flesh and firm texture, used for boiling, wedges and chips.

Maris Piper – creamy flesh and firm texture, used for boiling, roasting, wedges, chips and baking.

Vivaldi – white potatoes so creamy you can mash them without butter.

These are the characteristics of potatoes when cooked:

Floury potatoes are grainy and feel dry. They are best for mashed potatoes and shepherds pie.

Floury potato varieties: Estima, King Edward, Maris Piper, Desiree.

Waxy potatoes feel moist and pasty. They are used in salads as they stay firm and keep their shape.

Waxy potato varieties: Charlotte, Maris Peer.

New potato taste

| 1 | 2 | 3 | 4 | 5 | 6 | 7 | 8 | 9 |

Waxy ←——————————————————→ Floury

Waxy potatoes: translucent, moist feel. Stay firm and make great salad potatoes.
Floury potatoes: brighter, drier feel. Best for roast potatoes or mash.

Greener method of making mashed potato

Slice a large peeled potato to the thickness of a £1 coin. Place in a saucepan of boiling water and simmer for 5 minutes with the lid on. Turn off the heat and leave for 5 more minutes. Drain off the water, make sure the potatoes are dry, then mash with salt, pepper and milk.

Why is it green? Because you've used much less energy to cook the potato.

New potatoes

New potatoes come out of the ground early in the spring. You need to eat them as fresh as possible; just wash them and cook them in their skins.

63% water

32% carbohydrate

4% protein
1% other

Nutrition in a baked potato

Hotlinks

BBC Food

British Potato Council

To do

Find ten dishes from around the world that are made from potato, cassava, yam and sweet potato. Cook one of them for others to taste.

Cassava, yams and sweet potatoes

Cassava is one of the most widely used starchy root vegetables in the world. It can be boiled, fried and added to soups and stews. Cassava root flour is made into tapioca starch, which is used as a thickening, and fufu, a starchy dish popular in central Africa.

Yams are an important food in Africa, Asia and the Caribbean. Yam powder is like instant potato powder – just add water and it thickens.

The **sweet potato** came from South America. It has a pink skin and sweet taste when cooked, and can be boiled, fried or made into crisps.

Questions

1 What is meant by 'a staple food'?

2 What is the nutritional value of potatoes? What ingredients could you add to a potato dish to provide protein and other vitamins and minerals?

3 Which variety of potatoes would you use for a) mash, b) roast, d) wedges, d) baked potatoes?

4 How are cassava, yams and sweet potatoes cooked and served?

Pulses include beans, lentils and peas. A pulse is an edible seed that grows in a pod. India is the world's largest producer of pulses.

Different kinds of pulses

Nutritional value of pulses and beans

Pulses are a low-fat source of protein, fibre, vitamins and minerals, and they count as a portion of fruit and vegetables.

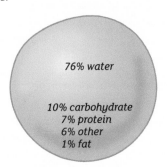

76% water

10% carbohydrate
7% protein
6% other
1% fat

Nutrition in a pea

This chart shows the nutrition in 100g of each of these pulses and beans.

Beans include butter beans, pinto beans, kidney beans, lentils, peas, and soya beans.

Some raw beans such as kidney beans and soya beans contain poisonous toxins, and the beans must be soaked for 12 hours and then boiled vigorously for 10 minutes before they are used in cooking to destroy the toxins. Canned beans have already been through this process so are safe to use from the can.

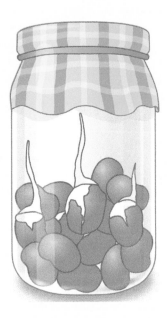

Sprouting beans

	Energy kcal	Protein g	Carbohydrate g	Fibre g	Vitamin C mg
Chickpeas	115	7.2	16	4.1	0
Lentils	105	8.8	17	3.8	0
Peas	69	6	9.7	5.1	12
Broad beans	81	7.9	11.7	6.5	8

Nutrients per 100 g

Soya beans are usually made into soya products, such as soya milk, tofu, TVP, and soya sauce (see page 72).

Whole **chickpeas** are used in salads and curry. Hummus is a dish of ground chickpeas, tahini paste, oil and garlic.

Lentils can be red, green, brown and yellow and make a delicious range of dishes used in Indian cooking, such as spicy dhal.

Baked beans are made from canned haricot beans in tomato sauce. Baked beans are cheap to make and buy and very nutritious. Heinz made its first tin in 1886.

Hotlinks

Heinz

Peas.org – information site provided by pea growers and processors

To do

Work in groups – each group has the job of promoting one type of beans. Tell the others how good your bean is, and make something tasty for them to try using the bean. Choose from this list:

Peas, chickpeas, broad beans, lentils – red, orange, yellow and green – black-eyed beans, butter beans, red kidney beans.

Baked-bean manufacturers also produce lower-salt and lower-sugar beans. Heinz makes Reduced Sugar and Salt Baked Beanz with 50% less salt and 25% less sugar than standard beans.

Peas

The UK is the largest producer of peas for freezing in Europe. Fresh peas are frozen within 2½ hours of picking. To serve them, no preparation is needed and there is no waste. Peas are very nutritious – they are rich in protein, carbohydrate and fibre, and low in fat.

When boiling frozen peas, add enough water to cover, bring to the boil and then cover and simmer for three minutes.

Mushy peas are dried marrowfat peas which have been soaked in water and mixed with salt, sugar and green colouring. They are often served with fried fish.

Peas being harvested

Questions

1 What is the nutritional value of beans and pulses?

2 Look at the chart opposite, which shows the nutrition per 100 grams. Which contains a) the most and the least protein, b) the most and the least carbohydrate, c) the most and the least fibre, d) the most vitamin C?

3 Explain how each of these pulses and beans are used in cooking: a) soya beans, b) chickpeas, c) lentils.

4 What safety precautions must you take if you are cooking some raw beans?

5 List three types of peas and explain how they can be cooked.

Soya beans are very high in protein, contain fibre, and much of the fat present is unsaturated.

Soya beans

Soya chunks

Uses for soya beans

Soya flour is used in bread and to increase the protein content of foods. Soya oil is used in margarine.

Soya foods include textured vegetable protein (TVP), soya milk, tofu (soya milk which has been set), soya sauce, miso, soya oil and margarine.

Soya milk is made by soaking soya beans in water. It is also made from soya flour. Soya milk has less fat than cows' milk and less saturated fat. It is a good source of protein. Some brands are fortified with calcium and vitamins. Soya milk provides an alternative for people who cannot drink cows' milk.

Textured vegetable protein (TVP) is soya flour which has been processed and dried to give a product that looks like meat and has a spongey texture. The texture is created by pushing the mixture through tubes (this process is called 'extruding'), drying it and then cutting into cubes or granules. It can then be used in recipes as a meat substitute.

Veggie burgers are often made from soya-based textured vegetable protein.

Tofu is soya bean curd, made by setting soya milk with calcium sulphate. Silken tofu is soft and creamy, and is used in dips and sauces. Firm tofu can be cut into cubes and absorbs the flavour of the cooking ingredients. It is used in stir fries and vegetable casseroles, where it provides protein. Tofu has been a really important food in Chinese and Far Eastern cooking for hundreds of years, and is a good source of protein.

Soya products

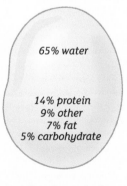

65% water

14% protein
9% other
7% fat
5% carbohydrate

Nutrition in soya beans

 **Recipe**

Make your own tofu.

Ingredients

For about 200g of tofu, you need:

500ml natural soya milk
1 tablespoon natural calcium sulphate – if using chemicals from the science department, do not eat this mixture.

Method

- Boil the soya milk in a saucepan to reach 100°C. Cool down to 70°C.

- Mix the calcium sulphate in 50ml warm water and pour slowly into the hot soya milk, stirring all the time.

- The mixture separates into white curds of tofu and liquid. Pour through a sieve lined with some muslin cloth, into a plastic container with holes which let the liquid drain out. A soft mixture of tofu remains in the container.

More uses for soya beans

Miso is used in Japanese cooking to give flavour to soups and stews. Miso is a fermented mixture made from soya beans, grain salt and water.

Traditional **soya sauce** was made by fermenting soya beans with wheat, salt and water, but most soya sauce sold today is made by a chemical process.

Soya oil and **soya margarine** are high in polyunsaturated fats and low in saturated fats, so they are recommended as healthier fats.

Soya burgers

GM soya

Genetically modified (GM) soya is grown in the United States. Ordinary soya crops use a lot of pesticides to prevent the plants from being destroyed by insects and other pests. GM soya beans need fewer pesticides. Labelling laws require food containing protein or DNA from GM soya to be declared.

 Further work

Gather more information on the nutritional claims for soya products.

 Hotlinks

Sustainweb.com – site of the campaign for better food and farming

The Vegetarian Society

 Questions

1 Make a list of the products that can be made from soya beans.

2 Describe how the following products are made a) TVP; b) tofu; c) miso; e) soya sauce. How is each product used?

3 What is the nutritional value of soya beans?

 To do

Carry out some research on the Internet and find 20 products which are made using soya beans.

Quorn mycoprotein

Quorn is a brand name for mycoprotein products.

1 The tiny plant that makes Quorn is a distant relative of the mushroom and grows naturally in soil.

2 The plant needs glucose, minerals, nitrogen and oxygen to grow. These ingredients are supplied to the **fermenter** where the plants grow rapidly.

3 After a few days, the Quorn is heat treated to stop it growing. Then the Quorn is made into thin, cream-coloured sheets with a wheaty taste.

4 Flavours and colours are mixed into the Quorn, then it is cut into slices or cubes.

5 Quorn can be used instead of meat for savoury dishes such as stews or curries.

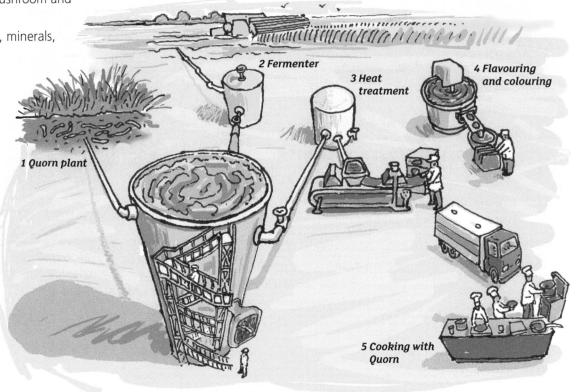

Steps in making Quorn

Mycoprotein is a food made by fermenting fungus, which is grown in a large fermentation tower. This is similar to the process of making yogurt. Oxygen, nitrogen, glucose, minerals and vitamins are continuously added and the mycoprotein begins to grow. When it is ready, the mycoprotein is 'harvested', which means it is filtered, drained and ready to be used as an ingredient in the manufacture of the Quorn range of products.

The mycoprotein is mixed with free-range egg white as a binder. The mycoprotein is textured to resemble meat and made into a wide range of products including mince, sausages, burgers and ready meals.

Nutrition

Mycoprotein is nutritious as it is low in fat and contains high-quality protein and dietary fibre.

It is suitable for vegetarians, but not for vegans as it contains egg white.

	Quorn	Soya mince	Minced beef
Nutrition information	Per 100g	Per 100g	Per 100g
Energy kJ/ kcal	397/94	370/88	934/225
Protein	14.5g	14g	20g
Carbohydrate	4.5g	4g	0
of which sugars	0.6g	0.2g	0
Fat	2g	0.2g	16g
of which saturates	0.5g	0.2g	7g
Fibre	5.5g	0	0
Salt	0.2g	4g	0

 Recipe for Quorn cottage pie

Serves 4

Topping

700g potatoes, peeled and chopped into chunks

1 large parsnip (200g), peeled and chopped into chunks

20g butter or margarine

Salt and pepper

Filling

1 small onion, peeled and finely chopped

1 medium carrot, peeled and finely chopped

1 tbsp vegetable oil

200g Quorn mince

100ml water

2 vegetable stock cubes

Method

- Heat the oven to 180°C, gas mark 5.
- Put the potatoes and parsnip in boiling water and cook until tender (15–20 minutes).
- Fry the onion and carrot gently in the oil until soft.
- Add the Quorn, water and stock cubes, heat and stir, then put in an ovenproof dish.
- Drain the potatoes and parsnips, mash, add butter and salt and pepper.
- Spread the topping on top of the Quorn mixture.
- Bake for 20 minutes until the top is golden brown.

Quorn cottage pie

Allergens: milk, egg

Net weight 1395g

	Per 100g	Per portion (348g)	% GDA* GDA
Energy kj	364.35 kj	1,270.67 kj	15.12%
Energy kcal	86.71 kcal	302.41 kcal	15.12%
Carbohydrate	3.64 g / 11.98 g	12.70 g	28.24%
of which sugars	1.90 g	41.80 g	18.17%
Total fat	3.00 g	6.62 g	7.36% ●
of which saturates	0.97 g	10.47 g	14.96% ●
Fibre	2.29 g	3.41 g	17.06% ●
Salt	0.70g	8.01 g	33.39%
Sodium	282.74 mg	2.46 g	41.08% ●
		986.07mg	41.08% ●

*Percentage Daily Values are based on a 2,000 calorie diet for an average adult. Your Daily Values may be higher or lower depending on your calorie needs.

This nutritional analysis of the home-made Quorn cottage pie has been created using a nutritional analysis program

74% water

15% protein
5% carbohydrate
4% other
2% fat

Nutrition in Quorn mince

 Hotlinks

Quorn website from Marlow Foods

 To do

Visit the Quorn website and find out about the range of products for sale. Why do you think people use this product in cooking? Find out about the nutritional claims.

Questions

1 What is mycoprotein, and how is it made and used as a food?

2 The chart on the opposite page compares the nutritional value of Quorn, soya mince and minced beef. Use the chart to explain the difference between the products – for example, beef has the most protein.

3 Look at the recipe for Quorn cottage pie. What would you serve with it to make a two-course meal? Give your reasons. Use the food label to help with your answer.

Table sugar is called sucrose and comes from sugar cane and sugar beet. Sugars are found naturally in other foods.

Natural sugars

- **Glucose** is found in fruits, vegetables and honey
- **Maltose** is found in barley
- **Lactose** is found in milk
- **Fructose** is found in fruits and honey

The history of sugar

The sugar-cane plant first came from India. People discovered how to extract sugar crystals from the cane juice and took these granules on sea journeys as they traded around the world. By the sixteenth century, the Caribbean had become the world's largest source of sugar, with huge sugar plantations grown on different islands.

In the eighteenth century, a scientist extracted sugar from sugar beet, a root that grew in the ground. Today, sugar beet supplies 30% of the world's sugar.

As a food, sugar provides 'empty calories'. It has no other nutrients, only carbohydrates as sugar for energy.

Sugar cane

Sugar beet

Sugar and tooth decay

Food and bacteria form plaque on the teeth. The bacteria in plaque break down sugars to form acid. This acid attacks the enamel coating of the teeth.

If the teeth are attacked too often, holes can form, leading to tooth decay.

It is therefore important to:

- avoid snacking on starchy, sugary foods through the day
- brush your teeth with fluoride toothpaste, which helps prevent tooth decay.

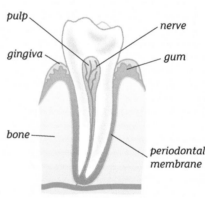

normal tooth   *tooth with cavity*

Sugar can cause tooth decay

Types of sugar

Granulated sugar is used to sweeten drinks and sweets

Caster sugar is used for baking

Brown sugars are used for flavour and colour

Icing sugar is sprinkled on cakes

Sugar in cooking

- Sugar makes food sweet.
- It makes jams and jellies by helping to preserve the fruit.
- It provides bulk in products such as ice cream, cakes and biscuits.
- It provides smoothness and flavour in products such as ice cream.

How much sugar is in a product?

It is easy to find the sugar content of a food product – look at the label.

This label shows nutritional information for chocolate brownies.

Chocolate brownies		
Nutrition information	Per 100g	Per brownie
energy	1720kJ	600kJ
	410 kCal	145 kCal
protein	5.7g	2g
carbohydrate	59g	21g
of which sugars	46g	16g
fat	17g	6g
fibre	4.5g	1.6g
salt	0.6g	0.2g

You can see that 46g out of 100g of brownie is sugar. To find the number of teaspoons of sugar, divide this figure by 5. These brownies are labelled 'high in sugar'.

Nutrition in sugar

Different types of sugar

@ Hotlinks

The Sugar Bureau – trade association for the UK sugar industry

To do

Most people need to reduce the amount of sugar they eat. Carry out some research and find how to lower the amount of sugar in food products. Design your own lower-sugar recipe: find a traditional recipe and try to reduce the sugar. Remember that sugar plays a role in forming the structure of cakes and biscuits, so you need to test the recipe. Carry out a nutritional analysis of your ideas to show that they have a lower sugar content.

Questions

1. List the five different types of natural sugars and where they are found.
2. Why do people say sugar has empty calories?
3. What is the difference between sugar cane and sugar beet?
4. How can sugary and starchy food cause tooth decay, and how can the decay be prevented?
5. How is sugar used in cooking? Give ten different ideas of your own.
6. How many teaspoons of sugar are found in chocolate brownies? Why is sugar used in the recipe?

Food packaging

Companies that pack and sell foodstuffs are trying to cut down on the amount of packaging used for food products. But we like our food to arrive in good condition, and to be safe to eat, so the right packaging is really important.

Why food needs packaging

If you put raw eggs in a paper bag they might break; the egg box provides protection, and also shows information.

Food needs packaging to:

- increase its shelf life and preserve it
- provide information
- protect the food from damage.

Different materials can be used for packaging:

- metals, which are very strong and don't break
- plastics, which are used for bags and bottles
- glass, which is used for jars and bottles
- paper and card, used for bags and cartons.

Recycling packaging

Food packaging makes up 30% of household waste, so we need to find ways to reduce this.

We need to think about the three Rs: Reduce, Reuse, Recycle.

1: Reduce the packaging

Some food products have far too much packaging.

Food can have a lot of packaging

Manufacturers are finding ways to make their packaging thinner, which will reduce the weight to be recycled.

2: Reuse the packaging

We can reuse some packaging for other purposes:

> **Carrier bags can be reused**
> **Glass jars can be used for storage**
> **Plastic tubs can be used as holders**

3: Recycle the packaging

More than 70% of our waste could be recycled, but we recycle only 30%. The rest goes into landfill, and we are running out of space for the landfill sites.

Waste packaging can be collected and reused, especially glass bottles and jars, plastic bottles, and cans.

However, most of the plastic waste that is recycled is sent to China, then comes back to us as recycled plastic bags.

Case study: Plastic-bag-free zone

Modbury was the first town to ban plastic bags.

In May 2007 all 43 shops in the Devon town of Modbury stopped handing out plastic carrier bags. After a six-month trial, Modbury has now become a permanent plastic-bag-free zone. Instead of using plastic bags, shoppers are asked to use 100% biodegradable alternatives made from corn starch, canvas, paper or cotton.

Modbury has banned plastic bags

Tips on reducing packaging

- Buy foods such as apples, potatoes and onions loose
- Take bags with you when shopping
- Look for biodegradable packaging on the things you buy.

♻	Mobius loop		Low-density		Green dot
	Glass		Recyclable steel		Board
(alu)	Aluminium	PETE	Polyethylene terephthalate	HDPE	High-density polyethylene

Symbols used on recyclable packaging

To do

Imagine what would happen if each of these foods was sold without packaging. Describe how you would carry them home and what might happen to each food along the journey.

Strawberries, eggs, biscuits, raw beef steak, olives, milk, chips, pizza

Draw and label the packaging that you would recommend for each food to keep it safe and clean.

How would you pack them?

Hotlinks

Waste Watch – an environmental charity

Waste & Resources Action Programme

Further work

Carry out a survey to find examples of the different materials used for food packaging. You can visit a supermarket or use the Internet to find information.

Questions

1 Not all food can be sold without packaging. Explain, with examples, why most food needs packaging.

2 List the different types of packaging used for food, and give examples of foods packed in these materials.

3 Write down ways to reduce the amount of food packaging. Describe the good and bad things about each of the ways.

Food is preserved to help it keep for longer and to stop it from spoiling. The different ways of preserving food stop the growth of bacteria, yeasts and moulds which make food go off.

Bacteria, yeasts and moulds

These micro-organisms need food, air, warmth and liquid to grow, so remove one of these things and the food will not go bad.

Drying removes the water in food, so micro-organisms cannot grow. Many fruits such as apricots, raisins and figs are dried as well as pasta and cereals.

Freezing freezes the liquid in food and turns it to ice. Micro-organisms cannot live without liquid. Frozen food will keep for a long time, but once the food is defrosted, it must be used quickly.

Vacuum packing removes all the air from the food packaging. Nuts and coffee are vacuum packed.

Salting and smoking are really old methods of food preservation. Bacon can be salted and smoked.

Sugar is used to preserve fruit. Jams are made from fruit and sugar.

Pickling uses vinegar, which is so acidic that the micro-organisms cannot grow in it.

Canning is a process where food is cooked in sealed cans or jars. The heat destroys the micro-organisms and the food is sealed so that it will keep for a very long time. Canned food usually comes in metal cans, but foil and plastic pouches and boxes can also be used to heat and seal food. UHT milk will keep for months and is sealed inside a carton.

Coffee can be vacuum packed

Tomatoes can be canned

Modified atmosphere packaging (MAP)

When you open a bag of crisps or some salad leaves, you may think the bag contains air. But this is in fact a mixture of gases which surround the food and increase its shelf life.

Fermentation is used to make beer, cheese and yogurt.

Chemical preservation

Chemicals can be added to food products to help them keep longer. They are listed as preservatives on the food label.

Design a dessert

Invent a dessert that is made from preserved foods:

Frozen – ice cream, frozen summer fruits

Dried – dates, apricots, sultanas, apples

Canned – mandarins, pineapple, pears

Sugared – jams, glacé cherries

Fermented – yogurt, fromage frais

Think of other preserved ingredients that you could use.

Further work

Find out more about the history of these different methods of preservation, and explain how each method helps the food to keep: a) drying, b) freezing, c) canning, d) smoking, e) pickling. Make a presentation of your findings.

To do

Suggest two other recipes like the dessert, which can be made entirely from preserved food.

@ Hotlinks

Canned food UK

Questions

1 Why do we preserve foods? Give examples of three foods that you know are preserved, and explain what makes them keep so long.

2 Answer the question using the chart below. Look at each of the pictures and describe how each food is preserved. List the foods in order to show which will keep for the longest time. Start with the one you think will only keep for a short time.

| Baked beans | Fish fingers | Pickled onions | Cheese | Sultanas |
| Bacon | Ice cream | Yogurt | Bagged salad | Jam |

Keeping food safe

Bad or decaying food can give us food poisoning and make us ill, so we need to shop for and store our food carefully to make sure it is safe to eat.

Shopping for food

Raw foods contain bacteria which can pass onto other foods, so keep raw foods – meat, fish, poultry and eggs, fruit and vegetables – away from cooked and ready-to-eat foods. Chilled and frozen food must be kept cold and stored quickly when you get home. Put chilled and frozen food in an insulated cool bag or box to keep it cold while you are transporting it.

Use a cool box for chilled and frozen food

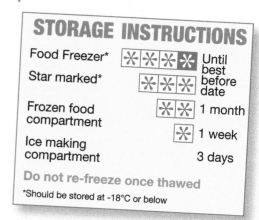
Storage temperatures for a fridge and a freezer

Storing food

If the food can be kept in a cupboard, make sure the cupboard is clean and dry, and free from pests. Storing food at room temperature is known as *ambient storage*.

The refrigerator

A refrigerator should be a safe place to store food.

The refrigerator should be kept at 3–5°C to store the food at a safe temperature. Test this with a fridge thermometer. If the refrigerator gets warmer than this, bacteria can breed and food becomes dangerous to eat.

Check the date codes on food, and get rid of out-of-date food.

Do not put hot food in the fridge, as this raises the temperature. Cool the food first.

Keep food covered and clean – the cover stops the food from drying out and also avoids cross-contamination.

Don't overfill the fridge, as this means cool air cannot circulate.

Fridge thermometer

Never store raw or uncooked food above cooked food – blood and liquid can drip onto the foods beneath.

Clean the fridge regularly – dirt and grime can get onto the food.

The freezer

Frozen food is kept in a freezer. The label shows you storage instructions. A freezer should run at -18°C or below, so check the temperature and defrost regularly.

Read the label

Packaged food has date codes on the label which tell you how long it will keep and how to store it.

Food labels tell you how long frozen food can be kept

STORAGE INSTRUCTIONS		
Food Freezer*	❄❄❄❄	Until best before date
Star marked*	❄❄❄	
Frozen food compartment	❄❄	1 month
Ice making compartment	❄	1 week
		3 days

Do not re-freeze once thawed
*Should be stored at -18°C or below

Use by: **06 JUN**

BEST BEFORE: **10/11/2008**

Use-by dates are for foods that can go off quite quickly. It can be dangerous to eat foods past their use-by date.

Best-before dates are for foods with a longer life. They show when food is at its best quality.

Throw away food that is past its use-by or best-before date.

Wash your hands before handling food

Our hands can pass bacteria and germs onto food, so wash your hands before and after handling any food. It is particularly important to wash your hands after going to the toilet.

This diagram shows the parts of the hands that are often missed when washing hands.

Bacteria spread more quickly if hands are wet, so dry hands thoroughly.

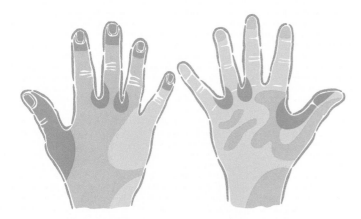

Back of hand   **Palm of hand**

▉ *Areas most frequently missed during hand washing*
▉ *Less frequently missed*
▉ *Not missed*

@ Hotlinks

Food and Drink Federation's food safety site

The Handwashing Leadership Forum

✎ To do

Find out how to wash your hands properly so they are clean enough to handle food.

This method is used by food factory workers to teach the importance of hand washing. They rub a tracer into their hands and view the hands under an ultra violet light. Areas that have been missed in washing show up in this test.

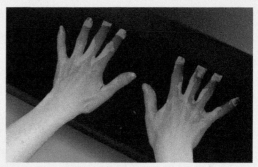

Hands under UV light

❓ Questions

1 Why is it important to store food safely?

2 What is the correct temperature to run a) a fridge, b) a freezer?

3 Make a list of five rules for safe food storage.

4 The mucky fridge shown here has some serious food disasters waiting to happen. Make a list of those you can find.

5 What is the difference between a use-by date and a best-before date? Give three examples of foods which might show each on a label.

Food hygiene and safety

The kitchen must be a safe place to prepare, cook and store food. You don't want dangerous bacteria to pass from a person or a food product and contaminate the food you are eating.

Rules to keep the kitchen safe and clean

- Wear clean aprons or protective clothing when working with food – this protects the food from the bacteria on your clothes.
- Tie back long hair and remove rings and jewellery – these can all carry bacteria.
- Wash your hands before and after working with food – your hands carry many bacteria.
- If you are ill with diarrhoea or sickness, do not work with food – the bacteria from these diseases can cause food poisoning.
- Don't cough, sneeze or spit near food – this passes on bacteria.
- Cover any cuts with a plaster – blue plasters are used in the food industry, so that they can easily be spotted.

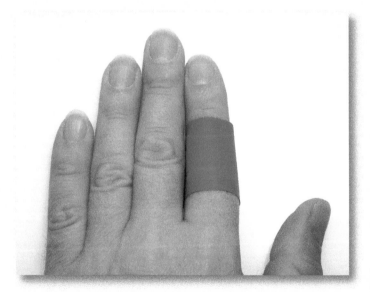

Keeping the kitchen clean

Food surfaces must be kept clean when you are preparing food.

Wash down work surfaces with a clean cloth or use an antibacterial spray which will kill bacteria.

Use clean tea towels and dishcloths. Old, wet dishcloths contain many bacteria.

Clear the rubbish – put food waste in a bin and empty it regularly.

Handling food

Keep raw and cooked food apart. The raw food can pass bacteria onto the cooked food. Prepare raw meat and fish separately – you should have separate chopping boards for these foods. Wash the equipment when you have finished, before you prepare other food.

Cooking

Cook all food until it is piping hot in order to kill bacteria. You can test the food with a temperature probe to see if it has reached 63°C.

Keep cold food cold and hot food hot!

Cooling food down

Let food cool before you put it in the fridge. A quick way is to put the food in a wide dish and stand the dish in a tray of cold water.

Kitchen hazards

Hazardous kitchen

Hazardous cook

Questions

1 Why it is important to keep a kitchen safe and clean?

2 Draw a poster called 'Safety and Hygiene in the Kitchen' to display in a food room.

3 What is meant by 'piping hot'?

4 Look at the pictures 'Hazardous kitchen' and 'Hazardous cook' above. List all the hazards you can find in each picture. Draw your own picture of a clean, safe kitchen and clean, safe cook.

Food temperature control

Food must be cooked and stored at the correct temperature; temperature control is really important to keep our food safe to eat.

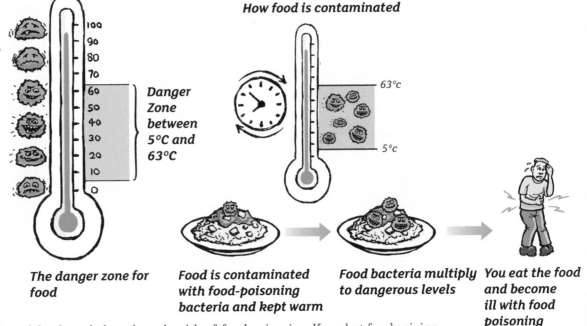

The danger zone

Food poisoning bacteria multiply best between 5° and 63°C. This is known as the **danger zone**. Most bacteria are killed at temperatures over 70°C, and bacteria do not grow, or grow only slowly, below 5°C. At very low temperatures some bacteria will die, but many survive and start to multiply again if warm conditions return.

Danger Zone between 5°C and 63°C

The danger zone for food

How food is contaminated

63°c

5°c

Food is contaminated with food-poisoning bacteria and kept warm

Food bacteria multiply to dangerous levels

You eat the food and become ill with food poisoning

Proper heating and chilling of food can help reduce the risk of food poisoning. Keep hot foods piping hot (above 63°C) and keep cold foods in the refrigerator until it is time to use them.

Keeping food cool

Food premises including shops and food outlets have very strict rules on temperature control in order to keep their food safe for customers. Chilled foods should be kept at 5°C or below. But which foods should be chilled?

These foods must be kept cool

Dairy products such as milk, yogurt, cheese, creamy desserts, cream

Uncooked pastry and dough products such as uncooked pizzas and pasta

Salads with prepared vegetables, bags of salad leaves, salads such as coleslaw, and products containing mayonnaise

Cooked foods including foods containing eggs, meat, fish, dairy products, cereals, rice, and vegetables

Food waiting to be served

Cooking and keeping food hot

If you cook food to over 70°C, you will kill most dangerous food bacteria. To be safe, you need to test the temperature using a food probe.

Many food service areas keep food warm to serve to their customers. They need to test the food temperature regularly to check that it is over 63°C, and not store the hot food for longer than two hours.

Cooling food down

If you want to keep a dish to be reheated, it needs to be cooled quickly. In a food factory they use blast chillers which can cool the food from 70°C to 3°C in 90 minutes. This picture shows food being loaded into the blast chiller.

In a kitchen, it is more difficult to lower the temperature of cooked food without a chiller. Cover the food and leave in a clean place near an open window. When cool, put in the refrigerator.

A blast chiller

These instructions show how hot food should be served piping hot

Reheating food

When you reheat cooked food, it must be piping hot at 63°C. Look carefully at cooking times on food packets – the manufacturers have tested the cooking time to make sure it reaches safe temperatures.

Below is part of a Food Hygiene Report on a café from the local Food Safety Advice Team. The owner must do these things by the next inspection or the café will be closed.

Food Hygiene Report

Your refrigerated food must be stored below 5°C at a temperature that will not promote the growth of pathogenic bacteria.

During cooking you must increase the core temperature of your sausages to a temperature that will destroy pathogenic bacteria – above 75°C for 30 seconds.

When keeping the sausages warm, you must keep them at a hot hold temperature of 63°C.

Your food must be kept at or below 5°C during preparation and above 63°C when cooked.

The temperature of this equipment must be checked daily and recorded: Refrigerators 1–4°C; Freezers -18°C to -22°C

? Questions

1 What is meant by the term 'danger zone', and why have these temperatures been chosen?

2 List ten foods which have to be stored a) in the refrigerator, b) at room temperature.

3 If you are cooking food, what temperature should be reached and why?

4 Make some rules for display in your classroom to explain how to cool, store and reheat food.

5 Read the Food Hygiene Report above. Describe the kitchen in this café. What do you think was going wrong? Try drawing and labelling the hazards in this kitchen.

Food safety: Activity

The previous pages explain the importance of food hygiene and safety in food preparation. Now that you know some of the rules, try to spot some of the mistakes in this drawing of the process of making baked beans.

Some clues

1 How are the workers dressed? What things need to be changed?

2 How is the food handled? What changes would you make?

3 What changes need to be made in the way the cans pass around the canning line?

4 What checks need to be made at each stage to make sure the ingredients are safe to use?

5 What things could go wrong in this factory?

Factory rules

Now design some factory rules to show:

• How the food workers should dress for work

• How they should prepare to handle food

• How the factory should be managed to avoid hazards

• How the ingredients should be checked before use

• How the beans should be packed and checked for delivery.

Answers

1 The workers have no hair nets and are wearing ties and jewellery, which would get caught in food. Overalls are undone.

2 They should not be handling food without wearing gloves. They should not be leaning over food, or tipping packets of food into tanks.

3 The cans are open to contamination and all the tanks are open to dust and pests.

4 The beans need to be handled hygienically, the tomato paste should go into a closed container, and the spices should be added from a container after checking. When the beans are cooked, there must be controls on the cooking and cooling temperature and the cans must be sealed properly.

5 The workers could drop bits of clothing and hair into the food. The machinery may not be clean as it is open to dust and pests. The spice packaging could drop into the food.

Making and packing baked beans

1 Dried navy beans are checked and cleaned. Broken beans are removed. Then the beans are tipped into large metal storage bins called hoppers.

2 The beans pass into a size checker which works like a giant sieve. Only the beans of the right size fall through the sieve.

3 The beans are then 'blanched' – washed and soaked in hot water to soften them and make them edible.

4 Clean, empty cans are filled with the blanched beans.

5 To make the sauce, large rollers squeeze tomato paste into a tank where water and special spices are added.

6 The sauce is heated with jets of steam, before being added to the cans.

7 The cans are then sealed with lids and go through a machine called a cooker which cooks the beans at a very high temperature and then cools them straight afterwards.

8 Hot air dries the cans so labels can be stuck on.

Tasting food

You need to taste food to see if it is good to eat. You can also use taste tests by asking other people for their views when deciding whether your recipes need changing.

Describing food

The ways to describe a food product, including its appearance, colour, texture, taste and aroma, are called **sensory analysis**.

Tasting rules

- Make sure that the food is safe to eat. Keep chilled food cool.
- Warn people if food contains nuts.
- Check individual food choices. Many religions have dietary rules which limit their food choices. For example, Muslims don't eat pork. Vegetarians don't eat food from animals.
- Wash your hands before you work with food.

Taste the difference

Food companies ask the public for their views of new products to see which tastes best.

Coca Cola and Pepsi Cola often ask people to tell the difference. Try this for yourself – it must be a fair test.

You need:

A bottle each of Coca Cola and Pepsi Cola – both at the same temperature

Glasses

Paper and pens to record results

Method

- Serve the drinks in similar glasses at the same temperature.
- Do not tell people which cola is which.
- Ask them to say which they like best and record the results.
- This is called a 'blind taste' test.
- Now carry out the test again and tell people which drink is which. Record the results.
- What is the difference between the test results? Why do you think a blind test is important for fair testing?

Set up a tasting panel

Star profile

The star profile is a useful tool to describe the taste and look of a food. Use words like the ones below to describe the flavour, how it looks and the texture of the food.

Tasting words

Flavour	Texture	How it looks
Fatty, salty, sharp, sour, spicy, sweet, tangy, tasty	Chewy, cold, crisp, firm, foamy, hard, juicy, sticky, tough, watery	Crunchy, dry, greasy, hot, moist, smooth, soggy

You can draw a star profile with four to eight words.

Method

Choose a product to make a star profile, for example a carrot.

You could use words such as *hard*, *sweet*, *crunchy*, *fresh*, *bright orange*.

Give each word a mark out of 5, where 5 means 'very' and 1 means 'not at all'.

So the carrot star profile looks like this:

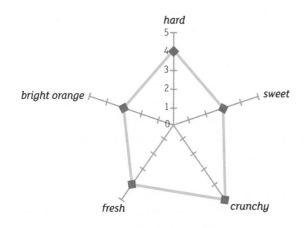

Star profile of a carrot

Questions

1 Draw a star profile for these foods:

Orange	**Chocolate biscuit**	**Apple**	**Fruit yogurt**	**Fried chicken**

You need to choose tasting words and then give each word a mark out of 5.
You can use a computer program such as Microsoft Excel® to create the star profile.

2 Why do you think food companies carry out taste tests before they launch a product for sale?

Glossary of terms

These terms have been used in the book.

Additives Products added to food to give different qualities, such as preservatives and flavours.

Allergy advice Allergic reactions are caused by substances in the environment known as allergens which are listed on food labels.

Ambient temperature Room temperature.

Bacteria Small micro-organisms which may be harmful to food, or could be useful in the human body, such as those in bio-yogurts.

Balanced diet Eating foods which provide a range of nutrients to meet daily needs. The 'eatwell plate' helps to explain a balanced diet.

Biodegradable A product that breaks down by biological activity and returns to the environment.

Calorie (kcal) A unit of energy

Carbon footprint The total amount of carbon dioxide (CO_2) and other greenhouse gases emitted over the full life cycle of a product or service.

Cereals Plant seeds.

Danger zone Food poisoning bacteria multiply between 5°C and 63°C – the danger zone.

Date codes Use-by and best-before dates on foods to show when they should be used.

Diet Food eaten during the day.

Eatwell plate Food Standards Agency diagram to show the groups of foods people need, and the correct proportions for a balanced diet.

Energy The energy supplied by food enables us to move and function.

Fair trade Giving a fair deal to people who work in some of the poorest countries of the world.

FAIRTRADE Mark The 'seal of approval' which appears on products meeting fair trade standards.

Fermentation The process when yeasts convert sugars to give off carbon dioxide gas.

Fertilisers Products which are used to enrich the soil – often chemicals.

Fibre Indigestible parts of food, which are important for a healthy gut.

Five a day Campaign to encourage people to eat at least five portions of fruit and vegetables a day.

Food miles The distance our food travels from farm to plate.

Fortification Adding vitamins and minerals to foods to increase their nutritional value.

Free range Allowing hens and other farm animals outside to roam.

Freedom food RSPCA label that shows farming methods reach certain standards.

GDAs Guideline Daily Amounts, recommended amounts that are shown on food labels.

Ghee Clarified butter.

Gluten Stretchy protein found in flour.

GM (genetically modified) Plants or animals are changed by altering their DNA to make them more resistant to drought, or to improve their growth.

Halal Food that is prepared according to Islamic principles.

Hazard Anything that can cause harm or danger.

Healthy eating pyramid A pyramid diagram used to show diet planning.

Homogenised milk Milk that has been through the homogenisation process, which breaks down the fat globules.

In season At the season when something grows locally – English apples are ready in the autumn.

Kosher Food that meets Jewish dietary laws.

Macronutrients The main nutrients found in food – carbohydrates, protein and fats

MAP Modified atmosphere packaging – the gases in the packaging have been changed to increase the shelf life of the food.

Micronutrients Nutrients found in small quantities in food, such as vitamins and minerals.

Mycoprotein A food made by fermenting fungus.

Nutrients The parts of food that keep the human body alive and healthy.

Organic food Food that meets strict standards for use of pesticides, additives, animal welfare and sustainability.

Paneer Cheese which comes from northern India.

Pasta Durum wheat and water made into a paste which becomes pasta.

Pasteurised A process of heating to kill harmful micro-organisms such as bacteria, yeasts and moulds.

Pathogenic Harmful or causing disease.

Pesticides Chemicals used to kill pests, especially insects.

Preservation Ways to help food keep longer.

Pulses Type of food that includes beans, lentils and peas.

Quorn A food product made from mycoprotein.

Raising agents Products that make food rise – such as yeast in bread.

Recyclable Things that can be used again – for example, certain types of packaging.

Red tractor Food symbol to show standards of farming and production have been met.

Salmonella A type of food-poisoning bacteria found in poultry and eggs.

Sensory analysis Methods to describe a food product including appearance, colour, texture, taste and aroma.

Shelf life The length of time a food remains safe to eat and of good quality.

Staple foods Foods which make up the main part of the traditional diet, particularly of poor areas. Staple foods include potatoes, yams and cassava.

Star profile Method to show how a product looks and tastes.

Starchy foods Foods that provide carbohydrate, such as bread, potatoes and cereals.

Sustainability Using a process that can be maintained for a long time, for example in farming and food production.

Tofu Soya bean curd.

Traffic light system System of red, amber and green symbols to show whether food is high, medium or low in some nutrient.

TVP Textured vegetable protein made from soya flour.

Vegan A vegetarian who does not eat any food or food product from animals.

Vegetarian A person who does not eat any meat, poultry, game, fish, shellfish or crustacea, or their by-products.

Whole grains All the edible parts of the grain – the germ, endosperm and bran.

Yeast Micro-organism used in bread making.

Index